Earthly Reches for Eternal Rewards

Living for the home beyond the sky

Joseph K. Olugboye

GIFT PAGE

THIS BOOK IS A SPECIAL GIFT

TO………………………………………………..………………

FROM……………………………………………………………

THE OCCASION OF………………………..…….............…………...

DATE……………………………………………………………

IT IS A TOKEN OF OUR LOVE, CARE AND CONTRIBUTION TO YOU, WE HOPE THIS WILL ETERNALLY BLESS YOU AS YOU READ THROUGH IN CHRIST JESUS NAME

Publishing page
Unless otherwise stated all scriptures quotation are taking from the English Standard Version of the Bible.

ISBN: 9798716361294
E-mail: pastorjosworls@gmail.com
Call: +234 8051558858, 08135685805

DEDICATION

To

LATE PASTOR JAMES ADEBISI ADEYEMI

The memory of the righteous is a blessing,
but the name of the wicked will rot

ACKNOWLEDGMENTS

My special appreciation goes to:
GOD THE FATHER, THE SON AND THE HOLY SPIRIT: for teaching my hand to war and my fingers to fight

MY WIFE ASORE BIDEMI FAITH: For being a succor and a source of inspiration to me.

MY PASTOR (MRS) OLUYINKA ADEYEMI:Trusting the Spirit of God in my life and taking the responsibility of equipping me for ministry

MY MENTORS: For sharing your life with me

MY PARTNERS: Your given has help publish this book.

MEMBERS OF TSC BODIJA: For the fellowship we share

EVANGELIST GRACE NIKE OLUWOLE & MR MUYIWA FA-TODU: For taking time to do the editing of this work

OLUGBOYES: For standing by and encouraging me, Expecialy PASTOR SAM OLUGBOYE. Whose support has made this work a reality.

YOU: For laying hold on my book, I hope it will prepare you for the home beyond the sky.

Indeed, you all have made my life count, thank you, May the Lord rewards you in Christ Jesus name. Amen.

Contents

Chapter 12

BENEFITS & REWARDS IN TRADING YOUR EARTHLY RICHES FOR ETERNAL REWARD.

<u>FINAL WORD</u>

<u>THE AUTHOR</u>

<u>THE BOOK</u>

INTRODUCTION

How much of Earthly Riches do you have?

Every one keep acquiring the earthly riches which the Preacher says "it's vanity upon vanity" and never think of securing eternal reward. As good as it sound to be rich here on earth it has no effect on the heavenly home until you deliberately trade it for eternal reward.

Why rich on earth and enter heaven wretched?

Knowing the brevity of man's life, the vanity of the earthly riches and the conviction of eternal home, Joseph Olugboye in his providence writing presents to you how to invest your earthly riches for eternal rewards.

in this book you will learn the following sub topics among others.

*the earthly riches

*the incorruptible treasure bank

*how to give your earthly riches for eternal reward

*Reasons you must invest your earthly riches for eternal rewards.

*Earthly and heavenly benefits of trading your earthly riches for eternal reward.

The scriptures says **"buy the truth and sell it not"** This book in your hand is the truth you've being waiting for in this side of eternity, I present this book, fully convince that it will help you to invest your earthly riches for eternal reward, make you to enjoy the benefits thereof and prepare you to enter heaven a rich individual.

Chapter 1

UNDERSTANDING THE EARTHLY BANK

Do not lay up for yourselves treasure on earth where moth

And rust destroy and where thieves break in and steal[1]

Matthew 6 vs 19

Bank is a place where money is kept and traded with in order to yield interest in return and withdraw from when needed. On the other hand, it is a financial establishment that uses money deposited by customers for investment, pays it out when required, give loans with interest and exchange currency. With these two definitions, I want to believe that you have the knowledge of what a bank is about. There are five major functions of bank mentioned in the two definitions above; I will like us to examine them:

1.   Place where money is kept for security.

2.   Place where money is invested to produce interest.

3.   Place where money saved is required when needed.

4.   Place where currency is exchanged

5.   Place where loan is given to business men and women

Place where money is kept for security purpose: when you keep your money in the bank, you feel some certain peace of mind for the security of your money. Have this truth to yourself today that the insecurity of money is the grave of the owner. When something is wrong with your bank, you start running into trouble of how to get back your money; some people have not recovered from the problem caused by some banks in Nigeria during the time of Charles Soludo (2004). This is a lesson to the sons of man that saving money in unsecure bank is dangerous. Nevertheless, bank has the responsibility to ensure the safety of money kept with them.

Place where money is invested to produce in return an interest to the depositor: Every bank trades with money deposited in their custody to get interest back to the depositor. This is one of the reasons men keep money in the bank. It is of no use to keep money where no increase will happen to it. Banks own the responsibility to trade with the money kept in savings account to yield an increase to the depositor.

Place where money saved is required when the need arise: The money saved in banks can be withdrawn at any time when the depositor is in need of it. However it must be made known here that it is the money you save you will have access to withdraw from the bank. Withdrawer slip is made available for every depositor in case they are in need of their money. It will sound foolish when a man that owns no account with a bank enter into the banking hall and start fighting to get his money.

Place where currency is exchanged: Bank is an organization that own power and ability (license) to exchange currency. This means that they are permitted to change money of a country to another country's currency. Assuming you own an account with a bank and you want to travel to other country, your bank can help you change the money you own in your account to the currency of the country you are going.

Place where loan is given to customers to aid there business: Bank lends money out to their customers in other to help them achieve a set goal. The customers return this money little by little as days go by. This process is called "Loaning". There in, the bank generates interest in return.

PROBLEMS OF THE EARTHLY BANKS

There are several problems attached to the earthly banks, however let's stay within the scope of the word of God.

Do not lay up for yourselves treasure on earth where moth

And rust destroy and where thieves break in and steal[1]

Matthew 6 vs 19

THE INSECURITY OF THE EARTHLY BANK

Several times we heard of many atrocities in the banking sector of the world, these are signal to the wise that the bank here on earth is not secure. The word "insecure" means "not safe". Majority have entered into trouble because of the failure of their bank to perform its duties or responsibilities.

To believers, I think this should not be a new thing; it is just like pouring water into a basket.

The bible says:

Do not lay up for yourselves treasure on earth where moth
And rust destroy and where thieves break in and steal[1]
Matthew 6 vs 19

I had opportunity to meet a man who is a security engineer in one of the Nigeria's bank. I tried to ask him the mode of his operation which he explained; it is more than what I can share here. Then I saw through the understanding of God's word that, there is no bank under the earth that is secure for eternal saving. I am not saying that saving money in the bank is not good but it should be done with a sense of purpose.

MOTH

Do not lay up for yourselves treasure on earth where moth
And rust destroy and where thieves break in and steal[1]
Matthew 6 vs 19

A moth is an insect like a butterfly which usually flies about at night to eat up goods. You may think in your mind that what the bible is saying here is not relevant to money in the bank or goods in store houses, but I want you to know that when you keep money in the bank whether saving or current, gradually the bank of the earth will deduct their monthly maintenance charges from it, except the interest-earning deposits.

Moths don't eat goods at once, it will take time before you discover that your money is gradually getting reduced. That is moth in the bank, they will deduct from your money for any transaction you made. You can bear me witness of what I am discussing with you, and there is moth in your earthly banks. Can't you see?

RUST

Do not lay up for yourselves treasure on earth where moth
And rust destroy and where thieves break in and steal[1]
Matthew 6 vs 19

The brown substances that form on the iron or steel when it comes in contact with water or fall inside water is called rust, there are three effect of rust on the iron.

It makes Iron look big in size

It changes the color of iron.

It makes iron to lose its strength

When you have money in earthly bank, just as rust makes iron to look big, you begin to feel same way. Saving money in the earthly bank does not make a man big, it is deception of the devil to make you think that your savings in the earthly bank is your worth. It is a wrong perception.

"and He said to them take care and be on your guard

against all covetousness, for one's life

does not consist in the abundance of His possession"[2]

Luke 12 vs. 15

I remember when I was younger {in my teens}, having a bank account was one of my priorities. I got myself involved in selling handset, phone accessories and air times. My first salary was ₦3,000. Immediately I collected it, I went to the community bank to open an account with them. I was given withdrawal and depositor slip. One of my dreams came to reality, what joy in my heart! After some time I went there to withdraw my money, to my surprise, I could not get my money complete. However, there was some interest added but not up to what was deducted as the bank charges. Although I felt happy and great that I was operating a bank account as small as I was then. The truth here is that money is not your worth.

Rust changes the color of iron and make it lose it strength. Some have materials and properties they keep in the treasure room, time and chance will soon catch up with them (wisdom). The car you keep in your garage, that is not in use will soon start depreciating and becomes outdated due to nature. The wears will soon turn to be old school (out of fashion). These are changes brought by the rust to goods kept in earthly treasure room or bank.

Iron generally loses strength when it becomes rusty. This means that the money and goods you keep somewhere will soon lose their worth and value when time and chance overtakes them. I once heard a musician who sang this Apala music from Yoruba tribe of Nigeria

"Mole fi ₦1,000 fe,

Mole fi ₦1,000 fe

Obirin to dara to si niwa

Mole fi ₦1000 fe". [3]

Meaning that: "he can marry a lady with a thousand naira if she is beautiful and possesses good character". A thousand naira then is like a million today. God supernatural supplied all my needs during my wedding I had so little on me, which could not get anything done, if I should calculate the money I spent from my personal account it would be over ₦200,000.00. This day's a thousand naira cannot plait hair let alone marrying a lady. You see, that is the realities of life. What you keep redundant will soon lose its values and worth.

THIEF

A thief is a person who steals another person's property, especially by stealth and without using force or threat of violence. Thieves break in and steal in the earthly banks. Recently, I was at home listening to the news when I heard that a bank open and promise to give double of what customers have in their savings account as a loan after four months of saving money with them (patronage). When the 4th months elapsed, the customers went back to have the promised loan, on getting to the banking hall, they meet the gate of the place looked up and there is no trace of their address. Banks are running into problems because thieve are raiding, Thieves are breaking into bank's technology to steal. Do not forget that the insecurity of the earthly treasure is the grave of the owner and the bible says

"do not lay up for yourself treasure on earth

where moths and rust destroy And where

Thieves break and steal[1]

Matthew 6 vs 19.

Chapter 1 Appendix : [1]Matthew 6 vs 19 ESV. [2]Luke 12 vs 15 ESV. [3]Yoruba circular music.

Chapter 2

INSIGHT TO THE EARTLY RICHES

"The earth is the Lord's and the fullness thereof

The word and those who dwell therein"

Psalm 24 vs 1 to

The blessing of the Lord makes rich and

he add no sorrow with it

Proverb 10 vs 22

The earthly riches includes money, goods, wealth, treasure, influence that is entrusted to you by the Lord for the enjoyment of your earthly days and for the benefits of others, there in, you can exchange it for eternal reward. Let's exploit the earthly riches below.

Money is any item or verifiable record that is generally accepted as payment for goods and services and repayment of debts, such as taxes, in a particular country or socio-economic context. The main functions of money are distinguished as: a medium of exchange, a unit of account, a store of value and sometimes, a standard of deferred payment. Any item or verifiable record that fulfills these functions can be considered as money. In Ecclesiastes 10:19 NIV. The bible says "… money is the answer for everything". When God gives you money His intention is to make you a blessing to his kingdom. Remember some has the money but the money fails them at the point of need. Now that Gods allow money to answer to your need, you need to exchange your earthly money for eternal reward.

 Goods are materials that satisfy human wants and provide utility, for example, to a consumer making a purchase of a satisfying product. A common distinction is made between goods that are tangible property, and services, which are non-physical. A good may be a consumable item that is useful to people but scarce in relation to its demand, so that human effort is required to obtain it. In contrast, free goods, such as air, are naturally in abundant supply and need no conscious effort to obtain them BECAUSE God made it available. Personal goods are things such as televisions, living room furniture, wallets, cellular telephones, almost anything owned or used on a daily basis that is not food related. All these are entrusted to you by the lord who daily loads us with benefits "Blessed be the Lord, who daily loads us with benefits, even the God of our salvation" Psalm 68 vs19. Selah. KJV.

Treasure & Wealth is the abundance of valuable financial assets or physical possessions which can be converted into a form that can be used for transactions. It is also the collection of valuable things you own. Your ownership may be through the blessing of God over the work of your hand or an inheritance that was transfer to you. The important thing here is, it is in your care and you will give account of how you trade it. Remember it is the Lord that gave men power to make wealth. "but remember that the LORD your God gives you the power to gain wealth, in order to confirm his covenant he swore to your fathers, as it is today." Deuteronomy 8:18 CSB.

Until you understand this truth that, it is the Lord that gives power to make wealth you may never achieve something of eternal value.

Living life carelessly as if you own everything is a proof of the man that did not know the brevity of humanity, the day of reckoning and the day of rewarding. Folks live on this planet forgetting that there is a place above the sky, where men will give account of their earthly days and get the reward of what they have invested in the eternity. A friend once told me that as a bible lives in a womb for nine months and did not know what happens outside the womb but can respond to light, torch and sound in the same way we only have idea of what eternity will looks like through the light of God's word. The earthly treasure that God entrusted to you should help create your eternal reward; you can exchange your earthly riches for eternal gain.

THE HEART AND ITS RICHES

"For where your treasure is, there will your heart be also"[1]

One of the ancient and unchanging truths I have learnt on earth is the inseparable union between the heart and its treasure, our motives differs but the focus of a man's heart is towards his or her treasure. It is a true saying and is worthy of acceptance that "where the treasure of a man is, there will his heart be".

I was once a manager in a business enterprise, my boss was extremely committed to his business. Nothing went un-noticed. I concluded that the man has invested so much in that business and he could not sit back to see it collapse. The care you give and the value you place on a thing deter-mines how you treasure it. The word of God is real, it says "For where your treasure is, there will your heart be also"[1] Matthew 6 vs 21.

THE HEART

Heart in this context is defined as the desire of the mind, the things you think of at all time. When you don't have anything to think to live for. When you have treasure in the safe, the life you live become more meaningful to you because you have a duty to protect it. Wherever your treasure is, there the desire of your hearts will be"[2]Matthew 6vs 21 NLT[2]

THE FOCUS

Focus: is the act of concentrating on a target with all attention deployed to it. The focus of an individual is towards his/her investment. A mother will always look after the success of her child because that is the treasure God has given her, which is why she places great value on them. The reason you don't allow people toy with your eyes is because they are treasures to you and when you lose them, you cannot get it anywhere that is why you guard it. In the same way, it has been proved that men everywhere keep an eagle eye on their investment because they treasure is, the bibles says where your treasure is there will your heart be. I like to conclude this chapter by saying one of the way to be heavenly minded while you are still here on earth is to save your earthly treasure in heaven by this you will be heavenly minded.

"For where your treasure is, there will your heart be also"[1] Matthew 6 vs 21

Charpter 2 appendix

Matthew 6 vs 21 ESV.   2. Mathew 6 vs 21 NLT

Chapter 3

THE INCORRUPTIBLE TREASURE BANK

"… lay up for yourselves treasures in heaven,
where neither moth nor rust destroys and
where thieves do not break in and steal"

Possibly you have not heard of it or you had heard but it does not make a meaning to you, I want to specially call your attention to an incorruptible and well secure treasure bank where there is neither moth nor rust to destroy and where thieves cannot operate, I called it the heavenly Bank.

Be still and recieve the word into your soul:

"But lay up for yourselves treasures in heaven,
where neither moth nor rust destroys and
where thieves do not break in and steal"[1]
Matthew 6 vs 20

HEAVENLY BANK

I have been operating this bank account for years now and I have the testimony of how it operates, it is a bank that can never fail. The founder of this bank is God, the Father who is the beginning and the end, who owns the earth and the fullness thereof, who is just and faithful to His word. He says 'The silver is mine and the gold is mine,' Haggai 2 vs 8

The customers of this bank never grow hypertensive or bankrupt. The heavenly BANK will not deny you in times of need, the earthly network may be fluctuating and the earthly ATM may fail, this bank cannot fail you, the earthly bank may close 4pm daily and be off at weekends this bank is always at your service 365 days and night. Public holidays do not affect its operation. You would not need to go anywhere in search of service, this bank delivers to you anywhere any time. This bank does not remove bank charges instead, they augment what you put to your account with good measure, pressed down, shaken together and running over (abundance) will be credited to your account. This bank is called the heavenly bank.

> *"give, and it will be given to you. Good measure,*
> *Pressed down, shaken together, running*
> *over, will be put into your lap.*
> *For with the measure you use it will be measured*
> *back to you."[2]   Luke 6:38 ESV.*

The heavenly bank offers Heavenly blessing and the values that your money can not buy such as Peace, Joy, long life in prosperity, healing, sound health, access to God the Father, answers to prayers, authority that controls things on earth, Ideas that bring prosperity without trouble, instruction that guides one in the path of righteousness, Apart from these, there are glory and rewards awaiting those who get rich towards God, when they leave this world of sin the eternal reward is awaiting them. At the end part of this book I will be sharing with you the benefits of given up your earthly riches for eternal rewards.

JESUS IS THE MASTER KEY

"and He called to Him His twelve disciple and gave them authority over unclean spirit to cast them out and to heal every disease and every affliction"[3]

Matthew 10 vs 1

" I will give you the keys of the kingdom of heaven and whatever you bind on earth will be bound in heaven, and whatever you loose on earth shall be loosed in heaven"[4]

Matthew 16 vs 19

" whatever you ask in my name, this I will do , that the father may be glorified in the son, if you ask anything in my name, I will do it"[5]

John 14 vs13 to 14

"…whatever you ask the Father in my name, He may give it to you."[6]

John 15 vs16b

"…The Father loves the Son and has

placed all things in His hands.."

John 3 vs 34 NLT

Jesus our saviour is the key to this heavenly bank. Jesus says *"in that day you will ask nothing of me, truly, truly, I say unto you whatever you ask of the father in my name, it will be given to you."* In another place, *He says: "I will give you the keys of the kingdom of heavens* (treasure room of heaven) and whatever you bind on earth shall be bound in heaven and whatever you loose on earth shall be loosed in heaven." That means Jesus is the key to heaven. Everyone that believes in the sacrifice of Jesus and confesses Him as Lord, has access to the treasure room of heaven (heavenly bank). Whatever you need Jesus has the keys to it in His hand. The bible says "The Father loves the Son and has placed everything in his hands"[10]. He is the bread that came from heaven. Jesus says "But here is the bread that comes down from heaven, which anyone may eat and not die. 51I am the living bread that came down from heaven. Whoever eats this bread will live forever. This bread is my flesh, which I will give for the life of the world."[8] . Jesus is the answer to this world, The way, the truth and the life.[9] "Jesus answered, "I am the way and the truth and the life.

No one comes to the Father except through me." [9]. Jesus is the master key, to God's kingdom, when you have Him you have everything. I want you to understand what Jesus is saying here, " I will give you the keys of the kingdom of heaven and whatever you bind on earth will be bound in heaven, and whatever you loose on earth shall be loosed in heaven"[4] .

BELIEVERS ARE THE BENEFICIARIES & HEIRS OF GOD

A believer is someone who believed in the sacrifice made by Jesus the son of God, believed that Jesus died and God raised Him from the death and has confessed Christ as the Lord. The bible says:

"if you confess with your mouth, "Jesus is Lord," and believe in your heart that God raised him from the dead, you will be saved. For it is with your heart that you believe and are justified, and it is with your mouth that you confess and are saved." Romans 10 vs. 9 to 10 NIV. Such people find no other reason to live here on earth than Jesus. Jesus says *"As the living Father sent me, and I live because of the Father, so whoever feeds on me, he also will live because of me."*

John 6 vs 57 ESV.

A heirs is a person legally entitled to the property or rank of another according to the provision of the will, such individual as being designed to inherit and enjoy the benefits thereof. Jesus Says: The glory that you have given me I have given to them, that they may be one even as we are one, John 17 vs 22 ESV. Therefore Believers are the beneficiaries and the heirs of heavenly treasure.

"Now if we are children, then we are heirs-heirs of God
and co-heirs with Christ, if indeed we share in his sufferings
in order that we may also share in his glory."[7]
Romans 8:17

let me say emphatically here, that there is no amount of earthly reaches that can give you eternal life, hope of tomorrow nor access to the kingdom of God. What gives these is faith In the Son of God who came to die and rose again and has gone to prepare a place for those who believe in Him.in the next chapter I will be shearing with you how to inherit the kingdom of God.

Chapter 3 appendix

Mathew 6 vs 20 ESV

Luke 6 vs 38 ESV.

Matthew 10 vs 1

Matthew 16 vs 19 ESV

John 14 vs13 to 14

John 15 vs16b

Romans 8 vs 17

John 6:50-51 50

John 14:6

John 3:35

Chapter 4

BECOMING A JOINT HEIR WITH CHRIST

"Now if we are children, then we are heirs-heirs of God and co-heirs with Christ, if indeed we share in his sufferings in order that we may also share in his glory."[1]

Romans 8:17

In this chapter, I will be sharing with you ways by which you can become a joint heir with Christ (having eternal life). I have said there is a how to everything under the heaven and when you do not know how, you get a wrong result. The heaven and the earth are full of treasures both physical and spiritual, all are owned by God the Father. The scripture says the earth is the Lord's and all the fullness thereof. Jesus is the son of God and everything the father has as He given to the son.

"…The Father loves the Son and has placed all things in His hands.

36Whoever believes in the Son has eternal life…"[2]

John 3 vs 34 to 36 NLT

Jesus says " All things have been entrusted to Me by My Father."[3] the only way to become a joint heir with Christ is to believe in Him and share in His suffering (His suffering includes His purpose on earth must especially for you). The truth remains that the father has giving Him everything.

WAYS TO BECOMING A JOINT HEIR WITH CHRIST (having eternal life)

"For God so loved the world, that he gave his only Son,

that whoever believes in him should not perish but have eternal life.

John 3 vs 16

1. BELIEVE THE SON: It is not enough to come to this world and get certificate, wife, husband, children, money, properties, fame and power without Jesus. The Bible says "man's life does not consist in multitude of wealth he possessed". For what does it profit a man to gain the whole world and forfeit his life? Life becomes more meaningful when you have a genuine encounter with Jesus Christ (the Son of God), who gave Himself for our transgression and now "to all who did receive Him who believed in His name, He gave power to become the sons of God"[9](joint heir with the son). We came into this son ship of the Lord by believing and confessing Christ as the Lord. As the scripture says:

"... if thou shalt confess with thy mouth the Lord Jesus, and shalt believe in thine heart that God hath raised him from the dead, thou shalt be saved. For with the heart man believeth unto righteousness; and with the mouth confession is made unto salvation."[4]

Romans 10:9-10

I present Jesus Christ to you, believe and confess Him and you will see the glory of God. This is the first step to becoming a joint heir with Christ.

2. FOLLOW THE SON: You must determine to follow Jesus. It is not enough to accept the Gospel of Jesus

Christ without following Him. The call to the kingdom of God is a called to following Jesus. Jesus told the rich man to come and follow Him. This is how to be with the Lord, following Jesus is also learning from other believers who have been in faith before you. This is call discipleship.

"and Jesus said to him, if you would be perfect,

go sell what you possess and give to the poor

and you will have treasure in heaven;

and come and follow me"[5]

Matthew 19 vs21

You will also need to belong to a church where you will learn more about Christ and have fellowship with other believers. This is how to be with the Lord. Remember that the first reason Jesus called people is that "they might be with Him"

"and he went up on the mountain and called to him

those whom he desiredand they came to him. And he

appointed twelve (whom he also named apostles)so that

they might be with him and he might send them out

to preachand have authority to cast out demon"[6]

Mark 3 vs 13 to 15

When you relate the two scriptures above together, you will see the reason Jesus Christ told the rich man to "come and follow me". Even when you have accepted the sacrifice of Jesus Christ, you will yet need to follow Him to the end.

I have discovered that knowledge and virtue is transferred through intimacy. You are effective today because you get closed to a master. The result of what you do is a proof of the knowledge you have acquired during the time of following the master. Believers are called Christians because they were Christ like in character {Acts 11 vs 26}. So if you don't follow Jesus Christ who will you resemble?

Jesus said "Very truly I tell you, the Son can do nothing by himself; he can do only what he sees his Father doing, because whatever the Father does the Son also does". John 5:19 19.KJV. You will never get the right knowledge of God and manifest His power without following Jesus. Therefore a call to following Jesus Christ is important to all believers. You must place priority on it, this is the second step in becoming the joint heir with Christ Jesus.

3.   **SOULS HARVESTING** The word Soul as used in this context refer to People, while harvesting is the act of gathering crops in to a barn for means of storage. Therefore soul harvesting is the gathering of people into the kingdom of God. Satan came to the world with the strategy to

steal, Kill and destroy also with the act of deception which he has succeeded at, but God want all men to Himself. That is why he sent Jesus to save man from the coming destruction on the earth, for satan and his cohort are destined for destruction. Jesus therefore came to the world to save men and make disciples who will in turn spread the goodnews of God's salvation to the world at large and gather men and women to His kingdom.

This primary aim of God is achieved through preaching, teaching and making disciple of people who had accepted the goodnews of salvation that Jesus Christ brought to the world. To really prove our Love for God we must partake in his assignment, and this is how to share in his suffering as a heir of God.

"Now if we are children, then we are heirs-heirs of God and co-heirs with Christ, if indeed we share in his sufferings in order that we may also share in his glory."[1]

Romans 8:17

1. spreading the goodnews of salvation through teaching MATTHEW 28VS 20
2. spreading the goodnews of salvation through Preaching MARK 16 VS 15
3. Making disciple of all nation (those that believe the gospel of the kingdom) MATTHEW 28 VS 19
4. Gathering believers together for communion,

fellowship and worship (the church setting) LUKE 22 VS 19

5. Baptize them that believe the goodnews MARK 16 VS 15, MATTHEW 28 VS

6. Administer and manifesting the gift of the spirit to the world MARK 16 VS18

Let us hear from Jesus:

" Go into all the world and proclaim(Preach)

the gospel to the whole creationWhoever believe

and is baptized will be save

But whoever does not believe will be condemned"

Marl 16 vs 15

"Go therefore and make disciple of all nations,

baptizing them in the name of the father and

of the son and of the holy spiritTeaching them

to observe all that I have commanded you

And behold I am with you always to the end of the age..."[7]

Matthew 28 vs19 to20

"...lift up your eyes and see that the

field are white for harvest.

Already the one who reaps is receiving wages

and gathering fruits for eternal lifeSo that

sower and reaper may rejoice together..."[8]

John 4 vs 35 to 38

Following the scriptures above, you will have the full knowledge of the vision of Jesus Christ.

There is not enough time for this vision, hence we cannot waste a little out of it, souls are dying daily without being saved. You and I have a limited time to spend on the earth. So you had better make it count for the Lord and have your heavenly account credited. Store in a place where you will rejoice seeing your investment for God prospering and having fruits unto eternal Life (John 4 vs 36).

Get out of your comfort zone to win a soul for the Lord, you can join the harvesters' team (Evangelism team) around you. Invest your time and resources towards the salvation of a soul that you may not appear before God on the last day empty handed. This is one major reason Christ Jesus came in to the world. If you take heed to this, you are sharing in His suffering and exchanging your earthly riches for eternal reward.

Chapter 4 appendix

    Romans 8:17

    John 3 vs 34 to 36 NLT

    MATHEW 11 VS 27 ESV

Romans 10:9-10

Matthew 19 vs 21

Mark 3 vs 13 to 15

Matthew 28 vs19 to20

John 4 vs 35 to 38

John 1 vs 13

Chapter 5

GIVING EARTHLY RICHES
FOR ETERNAL REWARD

*"and Jesus said to him, if you would be perfect,
go sell what you possess and give to the poor
and you will have treasure in heaven;
and come and follow me"* [1]

Giving is an act of appreciating God for entrusting to you the earthly riches and making you a blessing to others, it is also a way by which we connect to unending provision for life and ministry. God has not created a nonentity, this means that everyone God created on earth has ability to give one thing or the other, even the poor has something to give, only if he wants to give. Life is in stages and men are in sizes, whatever position you find yourself, there is something you can give. It may be food stuff or something of high value to you and not necessarily be money; the truth is that everyone has something to give. Until you acknowledge that you can give something you will never emerge a blessing (giver). Whatever you give to the Lord here on earth with a right mind is working out eternal reward for you. That is why:

" Jesus said to him, if you would be perfect,
go sell what you possess and give to the poor and you will
have treasure in heaven; and come and follow me"[1].

Matthew 19 vs21

Apostle Paul also said something that justify this when he was appreciating those gift he received from Philippians church, He said

"Not that I am looking for a gift,
but I am looking for what may be credited to your account."

Phil 4:17-18 NIV

When he made mentioned of "…credited to your account" he was talking about giving earthly riche for eternal reward.

Let us examine six ways to "have treasure in heaven" and "credit your heavenly account" from here.

Giving to Project in the house of God

Giving to the Poor in the household of faith

Giving to your Parents

Giving to MINISTERS

Giving to the Blessed

Giving to the Strangers

1. GIVING TO PROJECTs IN THE HOUSE OF GOD

(1st way to having treasure in heaven")

This involves your contribution to the need in the church of God. Whatever your income is, you must plan the budget of God alongside with yours.

"And the LORD spake unto Moses, saying, Speak unto the children of Israel, that they bring me an offering: of every man that giveth it willingly with his heart ye shall take my offering. And this is the offering which ye shall take of them; gold, and silver, and brass,And blue, and purple, and scarlet, and fine linen, and goats' hair, And rams' skins dyed red, and badgers' skins, and shittim wood, Oil for the light, spices for anointing oil, and for sweet incense, Onyx stones, and stones to be set in the ephod, and in the breastplate. And let them make me a sanctuary; that I may dwell among them. According to all that I shew thee, after the pattern of the tabernacle, and the pattern of all the instruments thereof, even so shall ye make it..." Exodus 25 vs. 1 to the end

Whenever you notice a project going on in your church, kindly join hand together with your pastor to accomplish it.

Four things God expects you to bring to his treasure house:

1.   **Your Tithe:** Tithe is the ten percent of your income or the 10% of the yield of your investment. Those that are rich towards God do not get offended at this request of the Lord instead, they seek to bring more than required.

Bring the whole tithe into the storehouse, that there may be food in my house. Test me in this," says the LORD Almighty, " and see if I will not throw open the floodgates of heaven and pour out so much blessing that there will not be room enough to store it.[3]

Malachi 3:10

God promised to open the store-house of heaven to pour out so much blessing that there will not be enough room to store it. God is not a man to lie or the son of man that will repent, just hold Him at His word and you will experience his blessing.

2.   **Your offerings:** God expect you to freely give towards a purpose in His house, which can be money, materials, human resources and you efforts. Take note of this clause: **"of every man that giveth it willingly with his heart ye shall take my offering"[1]** so, whatever you want to give to the Lord let it come from

your heart, let it be deliberate and not grudgingly or with compulsion.

"And the LORD spake unto Moses, saying, Speak unto the children of Israel, that they bring me an offering: of every man that giveth it willingly with his heart ye shall take my offering. And this is the offering which ye shall take of them; gold, and silver, and brass,And blue, and purple, and scarlet, and fine linen, and goats' hair, And rams' skins dyed red, and badgers' skins, and shittim canwood, Oil for the light, spices for anointing oil, and for sweet incense, Onyx stones, and stones to be set in the ephod, and in the breastplate. And let them make me a sanctuary; that I may dwell among them. According to all that I shew thee, after the pattern of the tabernacle, and the pattern of all the instruments thereof, even so shall ye make it..." Exodus 25 vs. 1 to the end

Lastly on your offering, your offering makes God to dwell with you. "And let them make me a sanctuary; that I may dwell among them". When you see the child of the king, you will also see a royal symbol around Him, I remember on my wedding day the royal rod was present to prove to the world that I am from a royal family. For those that give offering to the Lord there is a spiritual mark upon them that attracts favor and blessing, it also protects them from evil: these are kingdom symbol all around them.

3.   **Your pledge:** God expect you to redeem your pledges and pay the vow you made in His house after you have enjoyed His benefit, if you are faithful to it, He makes you abound in his blessing.

When you make a vow to God, do not delay to fulfill it. He has no pleasure in fools; fulfill your vow. It is better not to make a vow than to make one and not fulfill it. Do not let your mouth lead you into sin. And do not protest to the temple messenger, "My vow was a mistake." Why should God be angry at what you say and destroy the work of your hands?[4]

Ecclesiastes 5 vs 4 to 6.

4.   **First fruits of all your increase:** God expect you to willfully give Him the first fruits of all your increase has He promotes and increases your status.

Honor the LORD with your wealth and with

the firstfruits of all your produce; ESV.

Honour the LORD with thy substance, and with

the firstfruits of all thine increase: KJV

Proverb 3 vs 9

There are other things you can do or be part of to save treasure with the Lord, I call these "SERVICE TO GOD" These includes; **Praying, Taking care of the sanctuary, Ushering in the church, God's praise singer**, **Serving at believers table, Sound engineer** {media department}, *Construction Engineer* {construction Department} **Accounting for the Church, Nursing for the church.** You know your area of specialization and your ability; kindly get involved, Pastors cannot do this works alone, God wants to reach out to people through you. Let's face it and give our earthly riches for eternal reward.

2. GIVING TO THE POOR (2nd way to having treasure in heaven")

The poor are people that have a little or no possession at all. Let me give you a better definition, the Poor is people you are better than in the land of the living. When you give to people like these you have deposited in your heavenly account

"whoever is generous to the poor lends to the Lord

And he will repay him for his deed"[5]

Proverb 19 vs 17

"Blessed is the one who considers the poor

In the days of trouble the Lord delivers him…"[6]

Psalm 41 vs 1 to 3

A rich young man came to the Lord Jesus in the book of Matthew 19 vs 16 to 22 asking Him "Teacher, what good deed must I do to have eternal life" and Jesus asked him to "go and keep the whole commandment" the young man then said " I have kept all the commandment, what do I still lack?" and Jesus replied him saying "if you would be perfect, go sell what you possess and give to the poor and you will have treasure in heaven and follow me" when the young man heard this he went away sorrowful for he had great possession.

Just two more things to do after keeping the whole commandment of the bible, the two things will make him have treasures in heaven, that is eternal reward: sell what he possesses, give it to the poor and he will have treasures in heaven.

"Jesus said to him if you would be perfect,

go sell what you possess and give to the poor,

and you will have treasure in heaven; and come, follow me"[1]

Matthew 19 vs 21

Sell what you have and give to the poor. Let me ask you

this question, can you sell what you have, give it to the poor and start following Jesus Christ? Can you let go of your earthly possession that others may survive?

Three important messages you must learn in this place are:

a.   The man has kept the entire commandment. (laws doesn't make man perfect)

b.   The man is rich on earth but not towards God. (His trust is in the uncertain mammon)

c.   Despite his earthly riches he has no treasure in heaven. (He has no eternal reward).

These messages are for you to take proper care of the poor around you most especially, those in the family of faith, those that follow Christ Jesus. Never depend on the uncertain mammon, when you give to the poor, you have given to the Lord and have proven that your wealth is not your making. Surely, the Lord will reward you both here on earth and in heaven to come.

3. GIVING TO MINISTERS (DISCIPLES) (3rd way to having treasure in heaven")

Giving to disciples implies giving to the ministers of the gospel. There are people who have given their time and life to preaching of the gospel. Many a time you heard them saying: "I made up my mind to be a preacher of the gospel of Christ." Some of these people (Pastors) are now engaging in what Apostle Paul calls 'tent making'. That is, getting a circular business in order to get their needs met and not to be a burden to others. Kindly support what they are doing, if you cannot go, you can support those on the field. Your act of giving will help them to take the Gospel to the unreached around the world and God will credit that to your account in heaven. Let us see the mind of God concerning this;

"Whoever receives you receive me and whoever receive me

Receive him who send me, the one who receive

a prophet because

He is a prophet will receive a prophet's reward

and the one who

Receive a righteous person because he is righteous person

Will receive a righteous person's reward.

and whoever gives one of these little

one even a cup of cold water

because he is a disciple, truly, I say unto

you he will by no means lose

his reward."[7]

Matthew 10 vs 40 to 42.

This is another way to participate in the sharing of the gospel of Jesus Christ on earth, give to those who have committed themselves to teaching, preaching, making disciples for God in the world. If you cannot go, then give to support those that are ready to go or you shoulder the responsibility of sponsoring ministers of the Gospel. Bringing this point to an end, I want to ask you which aspects do you want Christ Jesus to remember you for, or what heavenly reward are you expecting? If you give toward God you will have His reward here on earth and in the heaven to come.

4. GIVING TO YOUR PARENTS (4th way to having treasure in heaven")

When you give to your parents, you give to secure long life and old age prosperities for yourself, However, God commanded it, therefore, when you give to your parents, you are fulfilling the word of God

honor your father and mother,[8]Matt 19:19NIV

"For God commanded, 'Honor your father

and your mother,'and, 'Whoever

reviles father or mother must surely die. But you

say, 'If anyone tells his father or his mother,

What you would have gained from me is given

to God, he need not honor his father.'

So for the sake of your tradition you have

made void the word of God".[9]

Matt 15:4-6ESV

God is greatly interested in you caring for your parents. You do not need to count their fault to them, kindly forgive your parents and take proper care of them. Our God knows how to fight for you and defend your cause. A "God bless you" from your parent, is more than a thousand prayers on the mountain, Obedience is better than sacrifice.

5. GIVING TO THE STRANGERS(5th way to having treasure in heaven")

"And you shall not strip your vineyard bare,

neither shall you gather the fallen grapes of your vineyard.

You shall leave them for the poor and for the

sojourner: I am the Lord your God."

Leiticus 19 vs 10ESV

Strangers are immigrant in your community, God expects you to take care of them. This is called hospitality; the act of welcoming, receiving, hosting and entertaining guest. There are many examples of those that give to the strangers in the bible. This single act was one of the character that distinguish Abraham from others, God would not have spoken to him if he did not entertained Him. Remember Rehab the harlot, she found favour in the sight of God by this single act, when Jericho was to be destroy, she and her family was rescue. And the Bible says

"Do not forget to entertain strangers, for by so doing some have unwittingly entertained angels."

Hebrews 13 vs 2.

When you give to strangers the blessing flows back to you in an unexplainable way most importantly the missionaries who are strangers in your area, provide food for them, and give them land property for the planting of the church of God. If you have space in your house you can accommodate them, if you have a car that you are not using in your garage, it will also help their navigation. This is how you can exchange your earthly riches for eternal reward.

Chapter 5: appendix

Matthew 19 vs21

Exodus 25 vs. 1 to the end

Malachi 3:10

Ecclesiastes 5 vs 4 to 6.

Proverb 19 vs 17

Psalm 41 vs 1 to 3

Matthew 10 vs 40 to 42.

Matt 19:19NIV

Matt 15:4-6ESV

Leiticus 19 vs 10ESV

Hebrews 13 vs 2.

Chapter 6

GUIDS TO EXCHANGING YOUR EARYLTY RICHES FOR ETERNAL REWARDS

"Cast your bread upon the waters, for you will find it after many days Give a portion to seven, or even to eight, for you know not what disaster may happen on earth If the clouds are full of rain, they empty themselves on the earth and if a tree falls to the south or to the north in the place where the trees falls there it will lies. He who observes the wind will not sow and he who regards the clouds will not reap As you do not know the way the spirit comes to the bones in the womb of a woman with child, so you do not know the work of God who makes everything.[1]

Ecclesiastes 11 vs 1 to 5

ere are the steps that will guide you to deposits in the treasure room of God as well as operate the heavenly bank. These points that I will be sharing with you, will help you to get rich towards God and help you make demand from the treasure room of heaven and it will be given to you simply because you operate the heavenly bank

There may be time when you think of giving up doing good, these points will also help you by assuring you that you are not wasting your resources rather, you are getting rich towards God.

Cast your bread upon the waters, for you

will find it after many days

Give a portion to seven, or even to eight, for you

know not what disaster may happen on earth

If the clouds are full of rain, they empty

themselves on the earth

and if a tree falls to the south or to the north in

the place where the trees falls there it will lies.

He who observes the wind will not sow and he

who regards the clouds will not reap

As you do not know the way the spirit comes to the

bones in the womb of a woman with child, so you do

not know the work of God who makes everything.[1]

Ecclesiastes 11 vs1 to 5

Cast your bread upon the waters, for you will find it after many days means that whatever you give, though it may seems thrown away, you will have its reward sooner or later. Give a portion to seven, or even to eight, for you know not what disaster may happen on earth mean you should give generally and freely, not just to one person but as you have the ability. If the clouds are full of rain, they empty themselves on the earth, means when your giving has reached the heavens, you will be rewarded. and if a tree falls to the south or to the north in the place where the trees falls there it will lie, means you are useful, mostly where God has positioned you, let all that surround you enjoy the blessing of God in your life. He who observes the wind will not sow and he who regards the clouds will not reap means you should not let the challenges you face while involve with good deeds discourage you from giving. As you do not know the way the spirit comes to the bones in the womb of a woman with child, so you do not know the work of God who makes everything. In essence, you may never know how God will reward you but He will.

Let's go through it.

1. **TOTAL TRUST IN GOD**

Teach those who are rich in this world not to be proud and not to trust in their money, which is so unreliable. Their trust should be in God, who richly gives us all we need for our enjoyment.1 Timothy 6:17NLT

Total trust in God means depending on God for all of your needs. It is a state where you do not depend on your resources even when you really have the money in your earthly bank. Some folks have put their trust in money; they have forgotten that money can fail at any time. Some put their trust in wealth and have lost the knowledge that "a man's life does not consist in multitudes of his wealth." If God had blessed you in the land of the living, you don't need to put your trust in your possession, there is need for you to acknowledge God the giver, for making you to be what you are. By doing this, you will learn not to put your trust in your possessions

I bring God's word to the rich in this present age not to be haughty, nor to set their hope on the uncertainty of riches, but on God who richly provides us with everything to enjoy. Haleluyah!

> *"Command those who are rich in this present world*
> *not to be arrogant nor to put their hope in wealth,*
> *which is so uncertain, but to put their hope in God, who*
> *richly provides us with everything for our enjoyment.*
> *Command them to do good, to be rich in good deeds,*
> *and to be generous and willing to share.*
> *In this way they will lay up treasure for themselves*
> *as a firm foundation for the coming age, so that they*
> *may take hold of the life that is truly life."[6]*
> *1 Tim 6:17-19 NIV*

Therefore never put your trust in money or riches for they will fail instead, invest in to God's kingdom so that you may have the harvest at the end of the age. Do not be like a fool that Jesus described in His teaching, let study it together:

"And he said to them, "Take care, and be on your guard

against all covetousness, for one's life does not consist in the abundance of his possessions." And he told them a parable, saying, "The land of a rich man produced plentifully, and he thought to himself, 'What shall I do, for I have nowhere to store my crops?' And he said, 'I will do this: I will tear down my barns and build larger ones, and there I will store all my grain and my goods.

And I will say to my soul, Soul, you have ample goods laid up for many years; relax, eat, drink, be merry.' But God said to him, 'Fool! This night your soul is required of you, and the things you have prepared, whose will they be?'

So is the one who lays up treasure for himself and is not rich toward God."[7]

Luke 12:15-21 ESV

It is clear that the man called "Rich" here has his trust in this world and has forgotten God. Do not be like this rich man that is not rich towards God. Put God as your first priority in life and by this, you will have treasure saved for yourself in heaven while you are still here on earth.

2. NEVER WORK FOR MONEY

Money is a messenger that you ought to send on errand. Money in it real definition is anything that is generally accepted as a means of exchange for value

FIVE WAYS TO KNOW YOU ARE WORKING FOR MONEY.

"No one can serve two masters. Either he will hate the one and love the other, or he will be devoted to the one and despise the other. You cannot serve both God and Money.[8]

Matt 6:2424NIV

1.   When you engage in a service without a definite goal you are working for money

2.   When you are paid for a service and all you could do is to spend your money on food, drinks, clothes etc, you are working for money

3.   When you are paid and you take all the money to the bank without separating the Lord's portion, you are working for money

4.   When you cherish your money more than the work of God {Gospel}, you are working for money

5.   When you cannot spend your money wisely, you are working for money (not having control over spending)

Money should not be cherished to the extent of digging

ground to hide it, it should be handled wisely. It should be invested, Wake up, if you work for money you can never become rich, money should be spent by you.

FIVE WAYS TO AVOID WORKING FOR MONEY

"He who love money will not be satisfied with money, nor he who loves wealth with his income; this also is vernity, when goods increase they increase who eat them, and what advantage has their owner but to see them with his eye? Sweet is the sleep of a laborer whether he eats little or much,but the full stomach of the rich will not let him sleep"

Ecclesiastes 5 vs 10 to13

1.   Draw a goal for yourself and send money earned to achieve it for you. Proverb 16 vs 1a

2.   Let the effect of your money be known in promoting the gospel {invest in Gospel}.

3.   Make a saving based on vision {don't eat all of your income}.

4.   Be wisely generous with your money, putting God's purpose as first priority

5.   Enjoy the toil of your Labour. Ecclesiastes 5 vs 18 to

20

This is the message for you not to work for money; those who work for money are serving money while those who engage in serving God with their riches have rule over money. You are encouraged to serve God not money and then Money will serve you.

3. **DO NOT BE ANXIOUSE**

This is another guide to help you own account in heaven. When a man is too anxious, it turns him to be too possessive and when you are possessive, you gain poverty. What you are thinking of as impossible or you are asking "how am I going to do it?" God who created you has the solution and will take care of it. Anxiety therefore, is a devilish infection which you need to guard against.

When it comes to giving to the Lord's project or to the Gospel, Devil will start speaking to the heart of folks, such words like: "remember you have not gotten a car for your wife, you have not finished building your house, your business is going down, instead of you giving this money, can't you invest it?' But you can always give some other time". All these are anxiety and the best way to guard against it, is to put God as your first priority. Jesus says:

"Therefore I tell you, do not worry about your life, what you will eat or drink; or about your body, what you will wear. Is not life more important than food,

and the body more important than clothes? Look at the birds of the air; they do not sow or reap or store away in barns, and yet your heavenly Father feeds them. Are you not much more valuable than they? Who of you by worrying can add a single hour to his life? "And why do you worry about clothes? See how the lilies of the field grow. They do not labor or spin. Yet I tell you that not even Solomon in all his splendor was dressed like one of these. If that is how God clothes the grass of the field, which is here today and tomorrow is thrown into the fire, will he not much more clothe you, O you of little faith? So do not worry, saying, 'What shall we eat?' or 'What shall we drink?' or 'What shall we wear?' For the pagans run after all these things, and your heavenly Father knows that you need them. But seek first his kingdom and his righteousness, and all these things will be given to you as well. Therefore do not worry about tomorrow, for tomorrow will worry about itself. Each day has enough trouble of its own."[9]

Matt 6:25-34 NIV.

You have read it by yourself the word of the Lord concerning anxiety. The Lord will care for you says the word of God.

'Casting all your anxieties on him, because he care for you' 1 Peter 5 vs 7 ESV.[9]

You have to learn casting your cares upon the Lord. Personally, I love to testify here that God is faithful at every stage of my life, He knows how to make things happen for those that put their trust in Him. You had better learn how to trust in God who daily loads His children with benefit without finding fault.

"Blessed be the Lord, who daily loadeth us with benefits, even the God of our salvation"[10]

. Psalm68 vs 19 KJV

Five R-ways to avoid being anxious

Read about the faithfulness of God. *"Those who know your name trust in you. for you LORD, have never forsaken those who seek you." Psalm9 vs 10.*

1. Rely on the faithfulness of God.

2. Relate your needs to the father

3. Relax so that you can hear the father's voice. "Be still and know that I am God . I will be exalted among the nations, I will be exalted in the earth". Psalm 46 vs 10

4. Rightly think on the instructions you had received

5. Run with the instruction of the Father

4. UNDERSTANDING THAT DESTRUCTION AWAITS ALL EARTHLY INVESTMENTS

I have written many things at the beginning of this book on the topic "DESTRUCTION AWAITS EARTHLY INVEST-MENTS". By and by you will notice a change of inferiority on your earthly investment. Since you know this, it is wise to save where there is no moth nor rust neither destruction nor thieves break in and steal, for where your treasure is there will your heart be also. Remember that I wrote in the early part of this book that "the insecurity of a treasure is the grave of the owner". Matthew 6 vs 19 to 21.

5. GOD WILL NOT FORGET YOUR LABOUR

"I was young and now I am old, yet I have

never seen the righteous forsaken

> *or their children begging bread. They are always*
> *generous and lend freely;*
> *their children will be blessed.*[11]
> *Psalm 37:25-26 NIV.*

Whatever you give to God, He will never forget it. What you give to God will speak during your days and after you are no more. Here, I like to say that landmark memories never die, no matter how folks war {fight} against it, it will speak. The word, righteous, means a faithful individual, the one who have his time for God, the one who does not participate in wrong doing, the one who cheerfully give to the Lord will not be forsaken or forgotten.

During the earthly days of my late father, who died in the 2002, his work speaks for us his children. Though he never knew any of his children will become a minister of the gospel, he would harvest his farm produce (Yam, Maze, tomatoes, vegetable leafs etc), put it on our heads with instruction "carry them to my pastor and other ministers of the gospel. He did this several times in his days. One of those things that he did was allotting a portion of his land to the Church of God and notifying the king who happened to be my uncle that the property has been given to the Church in case of any future dispute

In 2013 I was a missionary to Ogun State, Nigeria, I needed a place to start the Vision {planting a church}, God used a man to give me a landed property to start with. and In 2015 I relocated based on God's instruction to Ibadan Oyo state of Nigeria. Also in need of where to start the vision of God, another person called me concerning an uncompleted building in Ibadan for the planting of the church". Is it not amazing reading the faithfulness of God? "I have never seen the righteous forsaken or his children begging bread". What you give today will speak tomorrow for you or your children. Count it a privilege when you are in position to give to the work of God or to the needy. God can do without you however he depends on you for this moment to carry out his assignment on earth, take it serious.

Read with me the Lord's saying concerning your labour of love in faith:

" Instead of their shame my people will receive
a double portion, and instead of disgrace
they will rejoice in their inheritance;
and so they will inherit a double portion in their
land, and everlasting joy will be theirs.

"For I, the Lord, love justice; I hate robbery and iniquity. In my faithfulness I will reward the mand make an everlasting covenant with them.

Their descendants will be known among the nations and their offspring among the peoples. All who see them will acknowledge that they are a people the Lord has blessed."[12]

Isa 61:7-9 NIV.

Knowing that God will not forget your labor for him, let this keep you more focused on the work. Note this, men may forget your good investment, of a truth, they may deliberately talk it out when folks try to refer to it, yet do not let this discourage you, you are serving God who will not forget your work of faith. in Isaiah 61:8 THE MESSAGE:

"Because I, God, love fair dealing and
hate thievery and crime,
I'll pay your wages on time and in full, and establish
my eternal covenant with you.[13]

I, the Lord, love justice .I hate robbery and wrongdoing.
I will faithfully reward my people's work. I will
make an everlasting promise to them.

Therefore keep this in mind that God will not forget your good works of faith.

6. .GREATER REWARD AWAITS YOU

There is reward to everything under the heaven, as long as the earth remains; there will always be a time to plant and a time to harvest. When you invest in God's vision, greater reward is awaiting you. God is not a man, He will reciprocate all of your giving towards Him. To everyone that gives, the bible says:

"... It will be given to you. A good measure,

pressed down, shaken together and running

over, will be poured into your lap.

For with the measure you use, it will be measured to you."[14]

Luke 6:38 NIV.

God is not unjust; he will not forget your work and

the love you have shown him as you have helped

his people and continue to help them[15].

Hebrew 6 vs 10 NIV

In concluding this chapter, I have given you seven principles that will guide and help you in getting rich towards God, the 8th principle will be discussed in the next chapter (Give to God not man). Here are the principles again:

Faith & love

Total trust in God

Never work for money

Do not be anxious

Destruction awaits earthly investment

God will not forget your labour

Greater reward awaits you

Giving to God not man.

May you become a giver who is rich towards God in Christ Jesus Name.

Chapter 6 Appendix

Luke 12:15-21 ESV

Matthew 6:2424NIV

Matthew 6:25-34 NIV.

Psalm68 vs 19 KJV

Psalm 37:25-26 NIV.

Isaiah 61:7-9 NIV.

(from GOD'S WORD Copyright © 1995 by God's Word to the Nations Bible Society. All rights reserved.)

Luke 6:38 NIV.

Hebrew 6 vs 10 NIV

Chapter 7

HOW TO GIVE TO GOD NOT MAN

*"Then the Lord spoke to Moses, saying: "Speak to the
children of Israel, that they bring me an offering. From
everyone who gives it willingly with his heart you shall
take my offering. And this is the offering which you shall
take from them: gold, silver, and bronze; blue, purple, and
scarlet thread, fine linen, and goats' hair; ram skins dyed
red, badger skins, and acacia wood; oil for the light,
and spices for the anointing oil and for the
sweet incense; onyx stones, and stones to be set
in the ephod and in the breastplate.
And let them make Me a sanctuary, that I may dwell
among them. According to all that I show you, that
is, the pattern of the tabernacle and the pattern of
all its furnishings, just so you shall make it".[3]
Ex 25:1-9 NKJV*

Giving your Earthly Riches for Eternal Reward means giving to God and not giving to man. This is the way to invest in the heavenly bank. Several people have been giving to man not God, despite giving to the poor, to God's work, to Pastors, to the needy and so on which I explained in chapter six of this book. Do not get confused, the simple truth to it is, when you are giving, count it as giving to God. You may give all of your possession and yet not to God. Until you put God in the position of the gift receiver you have not given to God.

TEN WAYS TO KNOW PEOPLE THAT GIVE TO MAN

1 They give and expect the reward of their giving from the person they gave to

2 They give and monitor the gift.

3 They give and request for their gift when there is misunderstanding.

4 They help and make themselves a god to the person they helped

5 They say some related words to "if not for me", "I made him what he is today"...

6 They give money and monitor how the receiver spends the money.

7 They think of your big or small possession before giving to you

8 They give to secure fame and pride for themselves

9 They give to make someone else look inferior

10 They give and do the proclamation to the public

TEN WAYS TO KNOW PEOPLE THAT GIVE TO THE LORD

1 They give without counting the cost

2 They give cheerfully

3 They give in obedience to the Holy spirit

4 They give sacrificially

5 They give solemnly without others awareness

6 They give without counting the fault of the receiver

7 They give according to the biblical injunctions.

8 They give without expecting reward from the receiver but from God

7 They cast their seeds wisely

10 They always have something to give

LOVE TOWARD GIVING

A giving that is generally accepted by God is done in LOVE, this imply that it is motivated by LOVE. When you give without love, it is like pouring water in the basket. God commanded every one that gives even if you are giving to your enemy, to be done in Love and this is what He has proven to us by sending Jesus to Human race. "For God so loved the world that He gave His only begotten son"[1]. Love must precede your giving not giving to attract love.

The bible says:

> *"If I speak in the tongues of men and of angels,*
> *but have not love, I am only a resounding*
> *gong or a clanging cymbal.*
> *If I have the gift of prophecy and can fathom*
> *all mysteries and all knowledge,*
> *and if I have a faith that can move mountains,*
> *but have not love, I am nothing. If I*
> *give all I possess to the poor*
> *and surrender my body to the flames, but*
> *have not love, I gain nothing.[2]*
> *1 Cor 13:1-3 NIV.*

It is worthy of note that one may give all of his/ her possession to the extent of surrendering his/her body for destruction but without love. This is an important issue brethren and must be address. How much do you love God?. When you claim giving to God and do not love, the Bible says you have gained nothing. So also it is when you give to people without love, thinking you have given to God, you have gain nothing. Even in the Old Testament, when God commanded Moses to collect offering from the Israelites, God added a clause: the one who gives with love shall you accept as my offering.

"Then the Lord spoke to Moses, saying:
"Speak to the children of Israel, that
they bring me an offering.
From everyone who gives it willingly with
his heart you shall take my offering.
And this is the offering which you shall take from them:
gold, silver, and bronze; blue, purple, and scarlet
thread, fine linen, and goats' hair;
ram skins dyed red, badger skins, and acacia wood;
oil for the light, and spices for the anointing
oil and for the sweet incense;

> *onyx stones, and stones to be set in the*
>
> *ephod and in the breastplate.*
>
> *And let them make Me a sanctuary, that*
>
> *I may dwell among them.*
>
> *According to all that I show you, that is,*
>
> *the pattern of the tabernacle*
>
> *and the pattern of all its furnishings,*
>
> *just so you shall make it".[3]*
>
> *Ex 25:1-9 NKJV*

Start by developing your love towards God not money and earthly riches, because they will fade away. I pray that the love of God will flow across your soul, spirit and body in Jesus Name.

GIVE THE BEST NOT THE FAULTY

Folks in church today sing this wonderful song without really knowing the meaning

> *I will give my best to the Lord*
>
> *Best to the Lord   Best to the Lord*
>
> *I will give my best to the Lord*
>
> *Best to the Lord Best to the Lord [4]*

God is not a beggar and you should not give the bad thing to those who beg from you. This is what some of us do most of the time, that makes God raise a replacement. Imagine the one who gives you an asset and now is giving you a privilege to invest in His project {Gospel} or to say, you want to return to Him in appreciation, you now go for the damage property in your house, the property that you have condemned is what you carrying to Him. This is an act of ingrate to the Lord.

God asked Cain in the book of Genesis chapter 4 vs 7: ... if you do well, will you not be accepted? Let us study this together:

Adam lay with his wife Eve, and she became

pregnant and gave birth to Cain.She said, "With the

help of the Lord I have brought forth a man."

Later she gave birth to his brother Abel.

Now Abel kept flocks, and Cain worked the soil.

In the course of time Cain brought some of the fruits

of the soil as an offering to the Lord.

But Abel brought fat portions from some

of the firstborn of his flock.

The Lord looked with favor on Abel and his offering,

but on Cain and his offering he did not look with favor.

So Cain was very angry, and his face was downcast.

> *Then the Lord said to Cain, "Why are you*
> *angry? Why is your face downcast?*
> *If you do what is right, will you not be accepted?*
> *But if you do not do what is right, sin is crouching*
> *at your door;*
> *it desires to have you, but you must master it."[5]*
> *Gen 4:1-7 NIV.*

Take proper note of verse 3. It says **"Cain brought Some of the fruit"** while in verse 4 **"Abel brought fat portions of the firstborn of his flock"**. Cain brought some fruits which can be interpreted as anyhow selection of fruits but Abel brought Fat portions. Which means the big and special portions of his produce. At the end, God accepted Abel's offering and rejected Cain's offering. Has God been partial? No. your gift to God will somehow determine, your love for God and how important heaven will attend to you in time of challenges, therefore give the Lord your best.

If you do what is right, will you not be accepted?

But if you do not do what is right, sin is crouching at your door;

it desires to have you, but you must master it."[5]

You don't have extra time to be useful for God than now;

you had better made it count for Him by doing the right things. If you do what is right, will you not be accepted also?

But he's already made it plain how to live, what to do,

what God is looking for in men and women.

It's quite simple: Do what is fair and just to your

neighbor, be compassionate and loyal in your love,

And don't take yourself too seriously —take God seriously.[6]

Mic 6:8

Chapter 7 Appendix

    John 3 vs 16

    1 Corinthian 13:1-3 NIV.

    Exodus 25:1-9 NKJV

    Contemporary Gospel music

    Genesis 4:1-7 NIV.

    Micah 6:8 ESV

Chapter 8

FAITH TOWARD GIVING

By faith Abel offered to God a more excellent

sacrifice than Cain offered.

Through this he was approved as righteous,

with God testifying concerning his gifts.

He still speaks through his faith, though he is dead.

Heb. 11 vs 4

Now faith is the assurance of things hoped for, the conviction of things not seen.

For by it the people of old received their commendation.[2]

Heb 11:1-3 ESV

When we talk of faith we talk of the attribute of the unseen God who created all things from nothing but The WORD. For man to please God, man must have assurance and conviction of this unseen God.

"And without faith it is impossible to please him,

for whoever would draw near to God must believe

that he exists and that he rewards those who seek him."[3]

Heb 11:6 ESV

Without you having assurance and hope in this unseen God, you cannot achieve anything that is spiritual. Banking with heaven is a spirit-based investment therefore, you must be able to walk with God of faith knowing that His words are true and He is the doer of the word of faith. So, faith is the assurance of things you are hoping for and its conviction. Thus, the conviction of things yet to be.

EFFECTS OF FAITH IN TRADING YOUR EARTHLY RICHES FOR ETERNAL REWARD.

"And what more shall I say? For time would fail me to tell of Gideon, Barak, Samson, Jephthah, of David and Samuel and the prophets— who through faith conquered kingdoms, enforced justice, obtained promises, stopped the mouths of lions, quenched the power of fire, escaped the edge of the sword, were made strong out of weakness, became mighty in war, put foreign armies to flight. Women received back their dead by resurrection. Some were tortured, refusing to accept release, so that they might rise again to a better life"

Hebrew 11 vs 32 to 35 ESV

I like to put you in remembrance of this, without you having faith toward God you will never achieve anything of eternal values. Naturally speaking, when you give to the poor, it is like a waste of resources but the word of God says "giving to the poor is lending to God." what a great investment! Is it not amazing? It is faith {Assurance, conviction and hope} in the unseen God that makes you believe in His word.

a.   Faith makes you a word doer

b.   Faith makes you to believe in the things of God

c..   Faith makes you a giver

d.   Faith makes you a harvester

e.   Faith makes you to do exploit

a. FAITH MAKES YOU A WORD DOER.

"What good is it, my brothers, if a man claims to have faith but has no deeds? Can such faith save him? Suppose a brother or sister is without clothes and daily food. If one of you says to him, "Go, I wish you well; keep warm and well fed," but does nothing about his physical needs, what good is it? In the same way, faith by itself, if it is not accompanied by action, is dead."[4]

James 2:14-17 NIV

It is faith that will make you practice what you read in the word of God {Bible}. The one that ignores the message of life {word of God} is typically an unbeliever. Several folks in the church today, when they hear the word of God, they feel happy but they have no power to perform {act} it and when they get out of the church, the burden of the world comes back upon them, all the words they have heard will be forgotten and its looks like they are back in to square one. If you are in this category, you need to pray this prayer "Father I believe, help my unbelief"

Whatever you hear or behold in the word of God is real and living and as well has power to create and duplicate itself. The word of God has never failed; it is folks that have no faith.

You must have faith in the word of God, if not all you have read in this book may end up not profiting you, for this word of salvation is foolishness to those that are perishing, but to them that are being saved it is the power of God unto salvation. Thus, the word works, it is living, it is active and sharper than any two edged sword. Faith makes you act on the word of God.

b.   FAITH LAUNCHES YOU INTO MEETING NEEDS

Faith is stepping into what God has done, what He is doing and what He will do. It is faith that makes you believe the unseen God who daily works miracles. That is why faith is said to be the assurance of things hoped for, the conviction of things not seen. Where ever there is faith, action must follow it. Faith without an action following it, is death

"What good is it, my brothers, if a man claims to have faith

but has no deeds? Can such faith save him?

Suppose a brother or sister is without

clothes and daily food.

16 If one of you says to him, "Go, I wish

you well; keep warm and well fed,

" but does nothing about his physical needs, what good is it?

In the same way, faith by itself, if it is not

accompanied by action, is dead."[4]

James 2:14-17 NIV

If you have faith in this God, you will work out all His instructions. The only way to show that you have faith is showing your works according to His word.

c. FAITH MAKES YOU A GIVER

By faith Abel offered to God a more excellent sacrifice than Cain offered.

Through this he was approved as righteous,

with God testifying concerning his gifts.

He still speaks through his faith, though he is dead.

Hebrews 11 vs 4

When you see a man that is too possessive, you have seen

a faithless man. Without faith, it is impossible to please the Lord, without faith you cannot obey the commandment of giving because, you would think of where you will get in return if you give up what is in your hand. "By faith Abel offered to God a more excellent sacrifice than Cain offered…" having the knowledge that God deserve the best and He is the source of his blessing. Read this as well:

It was by faith that Abraham offered Isaac as a sacrifice when God was testing him.

Abraham, who had received God's promises, was ready to sacrifice his only son, Isaac,

even though God had told him, "Isaac is the son through whom your descendants will be counted."

Abraham reasoned that if Isaac died, God was able to bring him back to life again.

And in a sense, Abraham did receive his son back from the dead.

Hebrews 11 vs 17 to 19

Faith makes you to give out even your best and only one, the evidence of lack of faith is been possessive.

"One person gives freely, yet gains even more; another withholds unduly, but comes to poverty."

Proverbs 11:24

Several people are in this group, where is your faith? Some will say "I don't have money to give now" meaning "I have money but the money that I have is not for you" I wonder what vision you are pursuing that is bigger and more important? What vision do you have that is more than salvation of humanity? It is total lack of faith, faith helps you give, therefore check your life, If there is any trace of faithlessness, you need to work on it and the way to grow in faith is by hearing the word of God.

**d.	FAITH MAKES YOU A HARVESTER**

" By faith Sarah herself received power to conceive,

even when she was past the age,

since she considered him faithful who had promised."

Hebrews 11 vs 11

When you give to the Lord in any of the ways earlier discussed in this book, you have credited your heavenly account. Definitely you must harvest but the way God designed harvesting in His kingdom is different to the earthly style. God organizes Harvest for all of us even where we have not sown or planted. Sometimes I wonder the kind of favor I receive from people. I often say "Lord I do not deserve this".

One day I went to drop my tithe with a man of God, who prayed for me but his prayer amazed me. He said, "You will enjoy the favors that your parents had sown". Take note of this, it may be the good works of your parent or what you have done, it will flow like living water to your direction.

Let me share this testimony with you, I hope it will encourage you. My late father gave a parcel of his land to a church in my town and went to the king to authenticate its transfer of ownership. I was still a secondary school boy who had not discovered his purpose in life. When I became a Pastor several people have willfully given me access to their landed property for church use. The word of God is true "I have never seen the seed of the righteous lacking" one way or the other the Lord will bring the harvest to your location. So it is by faith you will receive the promise of God for your life.

Let us talk about the harvesting of souls. Until you have faith In Jesus, you will not see or attach any importance to what Jesus Christ came into the world to do. No one gets committed to what he does not know or believe. This is the more reason you need faith in God. Read His word, believe His words, practice the word and it will work for you just as it is working for me. This assurance we also have in the Lord that there is reward for all our toil with God on earth and in heaven to come.

e. FAITH MAKES YOU TO DO EXPLOIT.

By faith he went to live in the land of promise,
as in a foreign land,
living in tents with Isaac and Jacob, heirs
with him of the same promise.
By faith Sarah herself received power to conceive,
even when she was past the age,
since she considered him faithful who had promised.
Hebrews 11 vs 9 & 11.

Exploits in life and ministry is not the work of prayer or praises, it is the work of faith in God. When you pray, the Lord hears and ideas are dropped into your mind. When you praise, the Lord intervenes by causing His majestic voice to be heard and the earth bring its increase for you, but When you have faith in God, all what you heard, read in the word of God and those ideas God dropped in your hart will begin to materialize because faith moves you in to action.

It is faith that makes you attempt great things though they may look fearful but faith in the word of God tells you, it is possible. By faith Abraham went to live in the land of promise, as in a foreign land, living in tents with Isaac and Jacob, heirs with him of the same promise. By faith Sarah herself received power to conceive, even when she was past the age, since she considered him faithful who had promised. Faith therefore is the secret behind sowing and reaping in God's kingdom without this, you will achieve nothing. The bible says:

"…But the people who know their God shall be strong, and carry out great exploits."[5]

Dan 11:32 NKJV

You may have money, houses, cars, properties and fame in this world and still enter heaven being poor an in wretched. The only way to inherit heaven being prosperous, is to own account with God in this your earthly days. Therefore, let faith in Christ Jesus and in the word of God have its full place in your heart.

Chapter 9

WHY YOU MUST INVEST YOUR EARTHLY RICHES FOR ETERNAL REWARDS.

"do not lay up for yourselves treasure on earth, where moth and rust destroy and where thieves break in and steal. but lay up for yourselves treasure in heaven, where neither moth nor rust destroys and where thieves do not break in and steal".[1]

Matthew 6vs 19 -20

While Jesus was in this world, He went up to the mountain and there he gave several important teaching of His ministry to the disciples. Let us examine one of His messages.

"do not lay up for yourselves treasure on earth, where moth and rust destroy and where thieves break in and steal. but lay up for yourselves treasure in heaven, where neither moth nor rust destroys and where thieves do not break in and steal".[1] Matthew 6vs 19 -20

Jesus started by saying, do not lay up treasure for yourselves on. It sounds like instruction and command. "do not lay up treasure" whichever way it appears to you, it calls for attention. Do you ever think of the reason Jesus said "do not lay up treasure for yourselves here on earth but lay up for yourselves treasures in heaven. I want to share with you the reasons Jesus gave this instruction.

1. SECURITY PURPOSE

Lay up for yourselves treasure in heaven,
where thieves do not break in and steal[1]

There is security in heaven, there is no room for rust and moth to destroy, thieves can never have access to heaven. Security means all the measure that are taken to protect a place, there is full protection in heaven than the thieves can break. Several people do not know a secure place to cast their seed, that is why they keep goods at home, money in the earthly banks, some will say after all, there is no harm coming to it, sometime they conclude that merely looking at it that they are satisfied. It is wrong!!! For in your own eye destruction will come upon it all, before then, why don't you keep it where it will be traded with to credit, your heavenly account, where there is no thief that can break in. The goods saved in heaven is safe from all harm and destruction that happens to the goods on earth. What I am saying is that you can pass it to someone who will appreciate God for such a gift you gave. Think about it!!!

There is no amount of money or properties we keep for ourselves in this world that can satisfy us like those in heaven. What do you think will happen to your earthly riches if your soul is requested from you today?

1.   Mismanagement of these resources

2.   Government can lay claim of ownership.

3.   Lawyer's manipulation

4.   Mismanagement by unknown people

5.   Bank may claim some of it.

6.   Your earthly extended family will claim some of them

A young man who happened to be my neighbor died, the wife told me "The family is requesting for the property of my husband {their son}". The man died leaving behind three children and a mother, but the family who did not know much or how they got those properties wanted to have possession of it. May you not die untimely death In Jesus' Name. But if the Lord say to you "come home and rest today. What can you say you have deposited in your heavenly home?

Wake up: a word is said to be enough for the sons of the spirit. Let this mind be in you, that our home is in heaven, we are strangers here in the earth.

2. HEAVEN IS OUR HOME, YOU ARE A STRANGER HERE.

Dear friends, I warn you as temporary residents and
FOREIGNERS TO KEEP AWAY FROM WORLDLY DESIRES
THAT WAGE WAR AGAINST YOUR SOULS[2]
1 Peter 2 vs 11 NLT

Who is a man that left his fatherland to a strange land to live and during his stay, will not make provision for his father land (home) towards his return. Such man will become a burden to his family upon returning, for he has no preparation for his return. But the one that have prepared will receive a warm welcome to his own apartment which he has prepared long ago during his stay in the foreign land. This is a wisdom for those who want to return home at the end of their journey on earth.

Every one that exists on earth is a stranger in it, without this truth in your heart; you may set your heart (hope) on earthly things. Home is a place of rest; where one enjoys all he had toiled for while on earth. No one works without returning home to rest. Home therefore is of great importance. Jesus says:

> *"In my father's house are many rooms If it were not so, would I have told you That I go to prepare a place for you …I will come again and will take you to myself That where I am you may be also[3]"*
>
> *John 14 vs 2 to 3*

God gives us the privilege to live here on earth and to choose for ourselves where we want to spend our eternity and make available different treasures for ourselves. The bible verse above is pointing to the promise Jesus made to believers about the home that is beyond this earth, a place where He went to prepare for those who believes in Him. To all who believe in him, this promise still holds (abounds) after your experience on earth, there is home prepared for you and you can from this earth, save for and save into that home. That is why Jesus says "Lay up for yourselves treasures in heaven, where neither moth nor rust destroys and where thieves do not break in and steal"

Apostle Paul wrote in his letter to the church in Corinth that:

"if in this life only we have hope in Christ, we are of all people most to be pitied".[4]

1 Corinthians 15 vs 19

**"if in this life only we have hope in Christ ,
we are of all men most miserable".[5]**

1 Corinthians 15 vs 19 KJV

*"And if our hope in Christ is only for this life,
we are more to be pitied than anyone in the word".[6]*

1 Corinthians 15 vs 19 NLT

Since our home is in heaven therefore, is it not important

to save treasures in heaven? wake up! a word is said to be enough for the sons of the spirit. Let this mind be in you that our home is in heaven, we are strangers here in the earth.

> *"the land of a rich man produced*
> *plentifully(God's blessing)*
> *and he thought to himself, 'what shall*
> *I do, for I have nowhere*
> *to store my crops'?*
> *and he said, I will do this: I will tear down*
> *my barns and build larger*
> *ones, and there I will store all my grains and goods.*
> *and I will say to my soul, Soul, you have*
> *ample goods laid for many years:*
> *relax, eat, drink, be merry*
> *But God said to him 'fool ! this night*
> *your soul is required of you,*
> *And the things you have prepared, whose will they be?*
> *So is the one who lays up treasure for himself and is not rich*
> *toward God."[7]*
>
> *Luke 12 vs. 16 to 21*

Dear reader, you need to learn and practice this lifestyle

today so that God will not liken you unto a fool that stored up treasures for himself and was not rich towards God. Your real home is with the Lord is not here on earth.

"For we brought nothing into the world,

and we can take nothing out of it."

1 Tim 6:7NIV

However do not forget that it is God who made you who you are today it was never your making. Let me remind you that your body is an old house of clay which will return to the ground while the spirit and you soul will be called home one day, before then make your investments towards God. Luke12 vs21. [7]

3.TO BE HEAVENLY MINDED.

Much has been said about this point but I still have this to say that the wise live with eternity in view but the fools spends their life time as if they will be here forever, forgetting that there is life after death. When you invest your earthly riches for eternal rewards, your mind will always think of heaven because your treasure is there, how pleasant it is to know that this world is not a permanent home and to live in that light. The heart will always be at home. for the scripture says

*"Wherever your treasure is, there the desire
of your hart will also be"[8]
NLT Luke 12 vs 34.*

The way to leave with eternity in view is to trade your earthly riches for eternal reward this is the wisdom

4.HAVING THE DAY OF REWARDING IN MIND:

The scripture says: "For we must all appear and be revealed as we are before the judgment seat of Christ, so that each one may receive [his pay] according to what he has done in the body, whether good or evil [considering what his purpose and motive have been, and what he has achieved, been busy with, and given himself and his attention to accomplishing].   2 Corinthians 5 vs 10AMP

"When the Son of Man comes in His glory, and all the angels with Him, He will sit on his glorious throne. All the nations will be gathered before Him, and He will separate the people one from another as a shepherd separates the sheep from the goats. He will put the sheep on his right and the goats on his left.

"Then the King will say to those on his right, 'Come, you who are blessed by my Father; take your inheritance, the kingdom prepared for you since the creation of the world. For I was hungry and you gave me something to eat, I was thirsty and you gave me something to drink, I was a stranger and you invited me in, I needed clothes and you clothed me, I was sick and you looked after me, I was in prison and you came to visit me.' "Then the righteous will answer him, 'Lord, when did we see you hungry and feed you, or thirsty and give you something to drink? When did we see you a stranger and invite you in, or needing clothes and clothe you? 39 When did we see you sick or in prison and go to visit you?' "The King will reply, 'Truly I tell you, whatever you did for one of the least of these brothers and sisters of mine, you did for me.'

"Then He will say to those on his left, 'Depart from me, you who are cursed, into the eternal fire prepared for the devil and his angels. 42 For I was hungry and you gave me nothing to eat, I was thirsty and you gave me nothing to drink, 43 I was a stranger and you did not invite me in, I needed clothes and you did not clothe me, I was sick and in prison and you did not look after me. "They also will answer, 'Lord, when did we see you hungry or thirsty or a stranger or needing clothes or sick or in prison, and did not help you?'

"He will reply, 'Truly I tell you, whatever you did not do for one of the least of these, you did not do for me.' "Then they will go away to eternal punishment, but the righteous to eternal life."[9]

Matthew 24 vs 31 to 46

In the process of accumulating wealth in a wrong manner, the fools will say "the birds can only flies with what he has eaten". When they want to squander that which they have accumulated, they make such statement like; "since we are ignorant of what comes tomorrow we will enjoy today's life to fullest." God is only being patient with men. If you are in this category, God expect you to repent and come to his saving grace. There is judgment for every one that did not embrace God's provision for salvation. The bible says "it is appointed for men to die once, but after this the judgment … Christ was offered once to bear the sins of many. To those who eagerly wait for Him He will appear a second time, apart from sin, for salvation." Hebrew9 vs 27 &28 KJV.

One of the primary purpose of this book in your hand is to get you reconcile to the Lord and guide you to exchange your earthly riches for eternal reward. Therefor you must stop leaving recklessly and embrace the truth that there is a day of judgment, a day of reckoning and a day of re-warding. Those that believed in the provision of God (Jesus Christ) "will not come into judgment but has passed from death into life",(John 5 vs 24.) they will only give account and get the reward thereof. When the unbeliever will go away to eternal punishment, and the righteous to eternal life, *"For we must all appear before the judgment seat of Christ, so that each one may receive what is due for what he has done in the body, whether good or evil". 2 Cor 5:10 ESV.* Where will you belong and what reward will you receive?

5.THROUGH YOUR GIVEN THE GOSPEL WILL GO to THE END OF THE EARTH.

God has design this since the day of Zechariah that the gospel will be spread abroad through prosperity, the bible says "Cry yet, saying, Thus said the LORD of hosts; My cities through prosperity shall yet be spread abroad;..." Zechariah 1 vs17 kjv in Jubilee Bible 2000 version it say, Cry yet, saying, Thus saith the LORD of the hosts, My cities through abundance of good shall yet be widened;... the city of God is the kingdom of God, the expansion of this kingdom comes through the preaching, teaching and making of dis-ciples who will go for mission. All of these need earthly resource in order to be effective. Therefore your given is a vehicle that will help us take the gospel to the whole world.

The impact of your earthly riches on the spread of the gospel includes:

"But how are they to call on him in whom they have not believed? And how are they to believe in him of whom they have never heard? And how are they to hear without someone preaching? 15 And how are they to preach unless they are sent? As it is written, "How beautiful are the feet of those who preach the good news!"

Romans 10 vs 14 to 17. ESV

Preaching,

Teaching

Making of disciple.

Metting needs

Chapter 8 Appendix

Matthew 6vs 19 -20

1 Peter 2 vs 11 NLT

John 14 vs 2 to 3

1 Corinthians 15 vs 19

1 Corinthians 15 vs 19 KJV

1 Corinthians 15 vs 19 NLT

Luke 12 vs. 16 to 21

NLT Luke 12 vs 34.

Matthew 24 vs 31 to 46

Chapter 10

MYSTERY OF SEED SOWING

"He has scattered abroad his gifts to the poor;his righteousness endures forever."

Psalm 37 vs 26(CSB)

Multiplication is the mystery behind seed sowing, for every seed that you send to the mouth, you sent it to its grave. Prosperity on earth is a product of seed sowing and harvesting. As the earth remains planting and harvesting will never cease. If you fail to sow your seed, you will be forced to harvest nothing.

TIME IN SOWING

There is a time for everything, and a season

for every activity under heaven:

a time to be born and a time to die, a time

to plant and a time to uproot,

a time to kill and a time to heal, a time to

tear down and a time to build,

a time to weep and a time to laugh, a time

to mourn and a time to dance,

a time to scatter stones and a time to gather them,

a time to embrace and a time to refrain,

a time to search and a time to give up, a time

to keep and a time to throw away,

a time to tear and a time to mend, a time

to be silent and a time to speak,

a time to love and a time to hate, a time
for war and a time for peace.[1]
Eccl 3:1-8 NIV

Folks must come to understand time and season on earth. If a farmer goes out to the field in dry season to plant sweet potato, when the time to harvest comes, will he harvest bountifully? No! He will have nothing to harvest. Why? he did not observe the time before planting the potato stem. If you are late in planting your seed in the kingdom of God, it may not meet the purpose God wanted to use it for, some of us delay in laying down our seed on God's altar even when the Holy Spirit lays it on our mind, such seed may not bring bountiful return but definitely it will return for God has promised to reward every labor. The bible says that the children of Issachar had the understanding of times and season. 1 Chronicle 12 vs 32.[2] This is the time God has been waiting to bless your seed therefore, give what He has entrusted to you. The fellow that is in need today and you close your eye against him may not need your help tomorrow.

Let us read this testimony, a true life story of a woman who lives in Abuja Nigeria, who offered to pick up the son of his neighbor from Ibadan to Abuja, got him a good job, a week later, the woman was flying back to Ibadan and had a plane crash leaving her own children behind, helpless, weak and feeble. The young man she helped took responsibilities over her children (biological children of the deceased), till they all graduated from higher institution, get good jobs and got married. This woman used her influence to help the boy without knowing that she would soon die. Though the woman is late but her works still speak for her, See! the bible is so complete, it says: "the one who showed mercy is a neighbor"[3] Luke 10 vs35 to 37 [3], this woman helped an ordinary boy to become great in time, not waiting till the next week. Why are you delaying to help God's people around you? Time and chance happens to everything on earth, today is your time and chance given to you by God, tomorrow may be too late. Therefore, sow your seeds in time, that your harvest may be bountiful and in season. You may also decide to fold your arms but God's word stands forever "I have been young and now I am old, yet I have not seen the righteous abandoned or his children begging bread. "[4]

TWO CATEGORIES OF MEN

There are two categories of men on earth:

The Sower

The Eater

A sower is the one who believe in the principle of giving either having or not, they always have something valuable to give without complained and the Lord always provides for their need. It was Bro Gbile Akani that said "prosperity is having what you need per time"[5]. If you choose to be a sower in God's kingdom, God will always provide your need beyond your imagination that you may be a blessing to others.

"He has scattered abroad his gifts to the poor; his righteousness endures forever." Now he who supplies seed to the sower and bread for food will also supply and increase your store of seed and will enlarge the harvest of your righteousness. You will be made rich in every way so that you can be generous on every occasion, and through us your generosity will result in thanksgiving to God.[6]
2 Corinthian 9:9-11. NIV.

God will always supply seed to the sower and increase your store of seed and will enlarge the harvest of righteousness (your giving) to the one that chooses to be a sower, such a one will always abound in all good things even in good works, and they always have something to give in support of the gospel. God loves them and defends them jealously.

The eater: this is an individual who eats all of the resources that flows to his direction. I mean he spends all the resources on himself and his earthly family. God always provides bread to the eater, if you choose to be one, but also note that our heavenly Father will always provide seed for sower. You have the choice to make either to be a sower or an eater. WISDOM

TESTIMONY OF SOME SOWER

Looking through the bible, there are varying testimonies of people who can be referred to as sower. Let us consider some:

EZEKIAH'S TESTIMONY

In those days Hezekiah became ill and was at the point of death. The prophet Isaiah son of Amoz went to him and said, "This is what the Lord says: Put your house in order, because you are going to die; you will not recover."

Hezekiah turned his face to the wall and prayed to the

Lord, "Remember, O Lord, how I have walked before you faithfully and with wholehearted devotion and have done what is good in your eyes." And Hezekiah wept bitterly.

Before Isaiah had left the middle court, the word of the Lord came to him: "Go back and tell Hezekiah, the leader of my people, 'This is what the Lord, the God of your father David, says: I have heard your prayer and seen your tears; I will heal you. On the third day from now you will go up to the temple of the Lord. I will add fifteen years to your life. And I will deliver you and this city from the hand of the king of Assyria. I will defend this city for my sake and for the sake of my servant David.'" [7]

2 Kings 20:1-6 NIV

LESSON FROM HEZEKIAH'S TESTIMONY

1. He prayed to the Lord in the face of challenges.

2. He reminded God in face of the challenges. "Now, O Lord, please remember how I have..." 2 Kings 20:3 ESV. What will you tell God you have done for Him in the face of challenges?

3. He had worked for God.

4. He was faithful both in works and in giving.

5. He always does what was good in the sight of God.

6. The Lord remembered all his good works. What will God remember you for?

7. The Lord healed Him. Will God find a reason to heal you?

8. The Lord promised safety to him and his household.

TABITHA'S TESTIMONY

Now there was in Joppa a disciple named Tabitha, which, translated, means Dorcas. She was full of good works and acts of charity. In those days she became ill and died, and when they had washed her, they laid her in an upper room. Since Lydda was near Joppa, the disciples, hearing that Peter was there, sent two men to him, urging him, "Please come to us without delay." So Peter rose and went with them. And when he arrived, they took him to the upper room. All the widows stood beside him weeping and showing tunics and other garments that Dorcas made while she was with them.

But Peter put them all outside, and knelt down and prayed; and turning to the body he said, "Tabitha, arise." And she opened her eyes, and when she saw Peter she sat up. And he gave her his hand and raised her up. Then calling the saints and widows, he presented her alive." [8]

LEASONS FROM TABITHA'S TESTIMONY

1. She was a disciple. (Are you under any leader for discipleship?)
2. She was full of good works. (How often is your good works?)
3. She was full of charity "…and showing him the coats and other clothes Dorcas had made for them". Acts 9:39-40 NLT. (What will people testified that you have done for them?)
4. Others prayed for her. (Who will pray for you in the face challenge?)
5. She was handed to them alive. "… calling the saints and widows, he presented her alive."

TESTIMONY OF THE SHUNAMMITE WOMAN

"One day Elisha went to Shunem. And a well-to-do woman was there, who urged him to stay for a meal. So whenever he came by, he stopped there to eat. She said to her husband, "I know that this man who often comes our way is a holy man of God. Let's make a small room on the roof and put in it a bed and a table, a chair and a lamp for him. Then he can stay there whenever he comes to us."

One day when Elisha came, he went up to his room and lay down there. He said to his servant Gehazi, "Call the Shunammite." So he called her, and she stood before him. Elisha said to him, "Tell her, 'You have gone to all this trouble for us. Now what can be done for you? Can we speak on your behalf to the king or the commander of the army?"'She replied, "I have a home among my own people."

"What can be done for her?" Elisha asked. Gehazi said, "Well, she has no son and her husband is old." Then Elisha said, "Call her." So he called her, and she stood in the doorway. "About this time next year," Elisha said, "you will hold a son in your arms." "No, my lord," she objected. "Don't mislead your servant, O man of God!"

But the woman became pregnant, and the next year about that same time she gave birth to a son, just as Elisha had told her. The child grew, and one day he went out to his father, who was with the reapers. "My head! My head!" he said to his father. His father told a servant, "Carry him to his mother." After the servant had lifted him up and carried him to his mother, the boy sat on her lap until noon, and then he died. She went up and laid him on the bed of the man of God, then shut the door and went out.

She called her husband and said, "Please send me one of the servants and a donkey so I can go to the man of God quickly and return." "Why go to him today?" he asked. "It's not the New Moon or the Sabbath.""It's all right," she said.

She saddled the donkey and said to her servant, "Lead on; don't slow down for me unless I tell you." So she set out and came to the man of God at Mount Carmel. When he saw her in the distance, the man of God said to his servant Gehazi, "Look! There's the Shunammite! Run to meet her and ask her, 'Are you all right? Is your husband all right? Is your child all right?'""Everything is all right," she said.

When she reached the man of God at the mountain, she took hold of his feet. Gehazi came over to push her away, but the man of God said, "Leave her alone! She is in bitter distress, but the Lord has hidden it from me and has not told me why." "Did I ask you for a son, my lord?" she said. "Didn't I tell you, 'Don't raise my hopes'?"

Elisha said to Gehazi, "Tuck your cloak into your belt, take my staff in your hand and run. If you meet anyone, do not greet him, and if anyone greets you, do not answer. Lay my staff on the boy's face." But the child's mother said, "As surely as the Lord lives and as you live, I will not leave you." So he got up and followed her. Gehazi went on ahead and laid the staff on the boy's face, but there was no sound or response. So Gehazi went back to meet Elisha and told him, "The boy has not awakened."

When Elisha reached the house, there was the boy lying dead on his couch. 33 He went in, shut the door on the two of them and prayed to the Lord. 34 Then he got on the bed and lay upon the boy, mouth to mouth, eyes to eyes, hands to hands. As he stretched himself out upon him, the boy's body grew warm. 35 Elisha turned away and walked back and forth in the room and then got on the bed and stretched out upon him once more. The boy sneezed seven times and opened his eyes. [9]

2 Kings 4:8-35 NIV.

LEASONS FROM SHUNAMMITE WOMAN'S TESTIMONY

1. She always urged Elisha to wait for a meal. (How often do you provide food for your Pastor?).

2. She makes and furnishes a room for Elisha in the upper room. (Do you care about the place your pastor is living?)

3. Her character made Elisha to seek to be a blessing to her. (watch your character toward your Pastor that may be your next source blessing)

4. The Lord gave her the fruit of the womb. "He who receives you receives me, and he who receives me receives the one who sent me. Anyone who receives a prophet because he is a prophet will receive a prophet's reward, and anyone who receives a righteous man because he is a righteous man will receive a righteous man's reward. And if anyone gives even a cup of cold water to one of these little ones because he

is my disciple, I tell you the truth, he will certainly not lose his reward."[19] Matt 10:40-42 NIV

5.   In the midst of her problem Elisha stepped in, (who will intercede for you in time of problem?)

Chapter 9 Appendix

Ecclesiastes 3:1-8 NIV

1 Chronicle 12 vs 32.

Luke 10 vs35 to 37

Psalm 37:25

TAPPING GOD'S RESOURCES FOR LIFE AND MINISTRY BY BRO. GBELE AKANNI

2 Corinthian 9:9-11. NIV.

2 Kings 20:1-6 NIV

Acts 9:36-42 ESV.

2 Kings 4:8-35 NIV.

Matt 10:40-42 NIV

Chapter 11

HOW TO ENJOY THE HEAVENLY BLESSING FROM HERE.

"For I, the LORD, love justice; I hate robbery and wrong doing .In my faithfulness I will reward my people and make an everlasting covenant with them."

Isaiah 61:8

Every believer who give earthly riches for eternal reward will enjoy the heavenly blessing which is more than earthly riches, these are rewards from the Lord who will not own man anything, He is faithful, he will reciprocate any good done towards Him. the scripture says:

"For I, the LORD, love justice; I hate robbery and wrong doing.

In my faithfulness I will reward my people

and make an everlasting covenant with them.[9]

Isaiah 61:8.

God has preference for those that gives towards Him, most especially when such individual is a believer, he gives them access to the treasure room of heaven. Access to the treasury of God is giving through Jesus. This is one of the benefits of the sons of God. In John 1 verse 12, the bible says; to him who receive him He gave power to become the son of God[1]. to everyone that receive Jesus and believe in His name he has given right to become the son of God. I also want you to know that a son is the hair to the property of his Father. Therefore, believers are the heir of God. When Jesus came to the world, He said

"I will give you the keys of the kingdom of heaven;

Whatever you bind on earth will be bound in heaven,
and whatever you loose on earth will be loosed in heaven."[2]

Matt 16:19 NIV

Heavenly treasury is loaded with all treasures you can ever think of, whatsoever you can imagine in your spirit is available there, and all of these treasures are available for your benefits. I like to say here, that, God does not only own the heaven but the earth, the word says "the earth is the Lord and the fullness there off"[3], "the thousands of the cattles on the hill are his"[4], and "the most high rules the kingdom of men and give it to whom He will"[5]. Thus, Our God owns the universe. As long as you can name what you need in accordance to His will, you will have it.

Five keys to enjoying the heavenly blessing.

➢ ASK ACCORDING TO THE WILL OF GOD

➢ ASKING BASED ON THE WORD

➢ REMIND GOD WHILE ASKING

➢ MAKE YOUR DEMAND IN FAITH, KNOWING THAT GOD IS FAITHFUL

➢ EXPECT THE HEAVENLY INTERVENTION

1. ASK ACCORDING TO THE WILL OF GOD: Several people ask and did not receive because they did not ask according to God's will, asking according to God's will mean you must ask in conjunction with what pleases the Father. The scripture (James 4:2-3) says: You want something but don't get it. You kill and covet, but you cannot have what you want. You quarrel and fight. You do not have, because you do not ask God. 3 When you ask, you do not receive, because you ask with wrong motives, that you may spend what you get on your pleasures. Whenever you ask a thing without putting God in consideration you have asked wrongly.[6] That is the reason majority in the place of prayer without answer. Is it possible that he who says ask and you will receive[7] will deny those who ask Him? No! One of the reasons behind asking and not receiving is simply selfishness.

Therefore, I encourage you to find out what the will of God is and base your prayer on it. If you own account in heaven and you ask God anything according to His will, He will do it. The bible says (Heb 6:10) God is not unfair. He will not forget the work you did or the love you showed for him in the help you gave and are still giving to other Christians. in another version it says; For God is not so unjust as to overlook your work and the love that you showed for his sake in serving the saints, as you still do.[8] ESV.

2. ASKING BASED ON THE WORD OF GOD: you must understand this truth in withdrawing from the heavenly treasury; you are a heir of salvation, the son of God and the beloved of God, the beneficiary of heavenly wealth, This truth will help position you to receiving from the Lord, For God is not so unjust as to overlook your work and the love that you showed for his sake in serving the saints, as you still do[8], also you will need to back up your request with His word. God cannot deny Himself.

3. REMIND GOD IN THE DAY OF NEED: God is faithful, He will not forget your labour of love, but you will need to remind Him in the day of need, if indeed you have been rich towards Him then you will experience His salvation. There is no two way about this, just remind him and I tell you, He is faithful to remember your labour of Love. Prophet Isaiah said it in this way:

8"For I, the LORD, love justice; I hate robbery and wrong doing .In my faithfulness I will reward my people and make an everlasting covenant with them.[9]

Isaiah 6 1:8

4. MAKE YOUR DEMAND IN FAITH: The bible says; let us

therefore come boldly to the throne of grace that we may receive mercy and find grace to help in the time of need.[19] It takes faith to go to God in boldness knowing for sure that He is the rewarder of them that diligently seek Him.

I remember a brother who heard that I was in a great need just immediately my wife was delivered of our first child. He called to request for my bank details and immediately transferred the money to me. Within the interval of months, he sent for me to join him in prayer that his Boss in the office laid some allegation against him and that He will be facing the Human Resources Panel in the following week, He further said, since he has been in the office, no one has ever escaped such allegation, that means he will be dismissed. I calmly asked him if he knew the allegation? He confessed he did it, but with the consent of his boss, Then I rebuked him and asked for mercy on his behalf. I also ask the father to remember when I was in need you used him for me, please Father let the case be cancelled and I heard Him speak softly to me that he is forgiven and that he will find favor with the Human Resources Department. I called him and told him that the case is cancelled and whatever be the outcome of the panel, it will be in his favor. Lo and behold it was so.

That is heavenly bank responding to a need. Just remind God in the time of need and you will get His response.

5. EXPECT THE HEAVENLY INTERVENTION: Always expect a response from the Lord. The Bible says in Psalm 37 vs 25 25I was young and now I am old, yet I have never seen the righteous forsaken or their children begging bread.[11] God will always show up in time of need for those who get rich towards Him, therefore, you don't need to be afraid God is faithful, He will not forget your labour of love, In due time, he will reward you.

Chapter 10 Appendix

John 1 vs 12 ESV

Matthew 16:19 NIV

Psalm 24 vs 1 ESV

Psalm 50 vs 10 to 11

Daniel 4 vs 32 ESV

James 4:2-3 ESV.

MATTHEW 7 VS 7

Hebrews 6:10 ESV

Isaiah 61:8

HEBREW 4 VS 16

Psalm 37 vs 25

Chapter 12

BENEFITS & REWARDS IN TRADING YOUR
EARTHLY RICHES FOR ETERNAL REWARD.

*"if you faithfully obey the voice of the Lord your
God, being careful to do all his commandments that
I command you today, the Lord your God will set you
high above all the nations of the earth. And all these
blessings shall come upon you and overtake you,
if you obey the voice of the Lord your God…"*

Deuteronomy 28 v 1 to14

THE EARTHLY BENEFITS

Benefits is never a reward however it is an advantage or profit gained from something, in another word, it is the various types of non-wage compensation provided to members of an organization in addition to their normal wages or salaries. Benefits are given to people in other to help them enjoy their reward.

Everyone that is rich towards God is entitling to the kingdom benefits. Kingdome benefits are the blessings we enjoy from the Lord as a result of our obedience to His word (faith in His word). As you keep to getting rich towards God the bible says,

"if you faithfully obey the voice of the Lord your God, being careful to do all his commandments that I command you today, the Lord your God will set you high above all the nations of the earth. And all these blessings shall come upon you and overtake you, if you obey the voice of the Lord your God. Blessed shall you be in the city, and blessed shall you be in the field. Blessed shall be the fruit of your womb and the fruit of your ground and the fruit of your cattle, the increase of your herds and the young of your flock. Blessed shall be your basket and your kneading bowl. Blessed shall you be

when you come in, and blessed shall you be when you go out. "The Lord will cause your enemies who rise against you to be defeated before you. They shall come out against you one way and flee before you seven ways. The Lord will command the blessing on you in your barns and in all that you undertake. And he will bless you in the land that the Lord your God is giving you. The Lord will establish you as a people holy to himself, as he has sworn to you, if you keep the commandments of the Lord your God and walk in his ways. And all the peoples of the earth shall see that you are called by the name of the Lord, and they shall be afraid of you. And the Lord will make you abound in prosperity, in the fruit of your womb and in the fruit of your livestock and in the fruit of your ground, within the land that the Lord swore to your fathers to give you. The Lord will open to you his good treasury, the heavens, to give the rain to your land in its season and to bless all the work of your hands. And you shall lend to many nations, but you shall not borrow. And the Lord will make you the head and not the tail, and you shall only go up and not down, if you obey the commandments of the Lord your God, which I command you today, being careful to do them, and if you do not turn aside from any

of the words that I command you today, to the right hand or to the left, to go after other gods to serve them."
Deuteronomy 28 v 1 to14

I have written in chapter 3 of this book that, "The heavenly bank offers Heavenly blessing and the values that your money can not buy such as Peace, Joy, long life in prosperity, healing, sound health, access to God the Father, answers to prayers, authority that controls things on earth, Ideas that bring prosperity without trouble, instruction that guides one in the path of righteousness," Apart from these, there are glory (crowns) awaiting those who gives their earthly riche for eternal reward while on earth. when they leave this world of sin, the eternal reward is awaiting them. Let exploits the benefits of given up your earthly riches for eternal rewards. Naturally, the following blessing will begin to follow you here on earth.

1. **Uninterrupted lifting:** '...the Lord your God will set you high above all the nations of the earth. 'Deuteronomy 28 vs1.

And the Lord will make you the head and not the tail, and you shall only go up and not down, if you obey the commandments of the Lord your God, which I command you today, being careful to do them,

Deuteronomy 28 vs 13.

2. **Unexplainable fruitfulness:** '...blessed shall you be in the field. Blessed shall be the fruit of your womb and the fruit of your ground and the fruit of your cattle, the increase of your herds and the young of your flock. Blessed shall be your basket and your kneading bowl...' Deuteronomy 28 vs 4.

3. **Undeniable victory:** "The Lord will cause your enemies who rise against you to be defeated before you. They shall come out against you one way and flee before you seven ways. Deuteronomy 28 v 7.

4. **Unexplainable deliverance** "Blessed is the one who considers the poor! In the day of trouble the Lord delivers him; the Lord protects him and keeps him alive; he is called blessed in the land; you do not give him up to the will of his enemies. The Lord sustains him on his sickbed; in his illness you restore him to full health." Psalm 41 vs 1 to 3

5. **Unlimited prosperity:** "And the Lord will make you abound in prosperity, in the fruit of your womb and in the fruit of your livestock and in the fruit of your ground, within the land that the Lord swore to your fathers to give you." Deuteronomy 28 vs 13

6. **Unrestrained blessing:** " The Lord will open to you his good treasury, the heavens, to give the

rain to your land in its season and to bless all the work of your hands. And you shall lend to many nations, but you shall not borrow." Deuteronomy 28 vs 12

7. **Untold name:** The Lord will establish you as a people holy to himself, as he has sworn to you, if you keep the commandments of the Lord your God and walk in his ways. 10 And all the peoples of the earth shall see that you are called by the name of the Lord, and they shall be afraid of you. Deuteronomy 28 vs 9 & 10

8. **Unexplainable Provision** "And my God will supply every need of yours according to his riches in glory in Christ Jesus." Philippians 4 vs 19

9. **Unexplainable Healing:** "Blessed is the one who considers the poor! In the day of trouble the Lord delivers him; the Lord protects him and keeps him alive; he is called blessed in the land; you do not give him up to the will of his enemies. The Lord sustains him on his sickbed; in his illness you restore him to full health." Psalm 41 vs 1 to 3

10. **Unexplainable Love.** Each one must give as he has decided in his heart, not reluctantly or under compulsion, for God loves a cheerful giver. 8 And God is able to make all grace abound to you, so that having all sufficiency[e] in all things at all times, you may abound in every good work. 2 Corinthians 9 vs 7

& 8.

11.   **Unquantifiable multiplication.** "Give, and it will be given to you. A good measure, pressed down, shaken together and running over, will be poured into your lap. For with the measure you use, it will be measured to you." Luke 6 vs 38

12.   **Uninterrupted peace:** how will you interpret this scripture? "Blessed is the one who considers the poor! In the day of trouble the Lord delivers him; the Lord protects him and keeps him alive; he is called blessed in the land; you do not give him up to the will of his enemies. The Lord sustains him on his sickbed; in his illness you restore him to full health."
Psalm 41 vs 1 to 3

13.   **Unstoppable power to enjoy wealth:** hope you will agree with me that several people has the money but the money cannot save them, such people lacks the power to enjoy wealth, this power is gift to those that have invest their earthly riches for eternal reward. The bible says "Behold, what I have seen to be good and fitting is to eat and drink and find enjoyment in all the toil with which one toils under the sun the few days of his life that God has given him, for this is his lot. Everyone also to whom God has given wealth and possessions and power to enjoy them, and to accept his lot and rejoice in his toil—this is the gift of God. For he will not

much remember the days of his life because God keeps him occupied with joy in his heart." Eccl 5:18-20 ESV

THE ETERNAL REWARD

Jesus says "Anyone who welcomes you welcomes me, and anyone who welcomes me welcomes the one who sent me. 41 Whoever welcomes a prophet as a prophet will receive a prophet's reward, and whoever welcomes a righteous person as a righteous person will receive a righteous person's reward. 42 And if anyone gives even a cup of cold water to one of these little ones who is my disciple, truly I tell you, that person will certainly not lose their reward."[1] Matthew 10 vs 40 to 42.

For everything you do, you give, either in service or material resources to the saints; God is set to reward you both in this world and in the word to come. "For we must all appear before the judgment seat of Christ, so that each one may receive what is due for what he has done in the body, whether good or evil". 2 Cor 5:10 ESV.

Jesus used this story to illustrate and ascertain your great reward: "Then the King will say to those on his right, 'Come, you who are blessed by my Father; take your inheritance, the kingdom prepared for you since the creation of the world. For I was hungry and you gave me something to eat, I was thirsty and you gave me something to drink, I was a stranger and you invited me in, I needed clothes and you clothed me, I was sick and you looked after me, I was in prison and you came to visit me.' "Then the righteous will answer him, 'Lord, when did we see you hungry and feed you, or thirsty and give you something to drink? When did we see you a stranger and invite you in, or needing clothes and clothe you? 39When did we see you sick or in prison and go to visit you?' "The King will reply, 'Truly I tell you, whatever you did for one of the least of these brothers and sisters of mine, you did for me.'

 "Then he will say to those on his left, 'Depart from me, you who are cursed, into the eternal fire prepared for the devil and his angels. 42For I was hungry and you gave me nothing to eat, I was thirsty and you gave me nothing to drink, 43I was a stranger and you did not invite me in, I needed clothes and you did not clothe me, I was sick and in prison and you did not look after me.'"They also will answer, 'Lord, when did we see you hungry or thirsty or a stranger or needing clothes or sick or in prison, and did not help you?'

"He will reply, 'Truly I tell you, whatever you did not do for one of the least of these, you did not do for me.' "Then they will go away to eternal punishment, but the righteous to eternal life."[2]

Mattew 24 vs 31 to 46

CROWNS TO BE EXPECTED IN HEAVEN *(DESIGNED FOR THOSE WHO GIVE THEIR EARTLY RICHES FOR ETERNAL REWARD.)*

Heaven is a place of rewarding, this means: it is where we will receive crowns of different types, the bible says

"behold I come quickly! Hold fast what you have, that no one may take your crow"

Revelation 2 vs 11

"For we must all appear before the judgment seat of Christ, so that each one may receive what is due for what he has done in the body, whether good or evil".

2 Corinthians 5:10 ESV.

1. The Incorruptible Crown (faithfulness in self-control)

1 Corinthian 9 vs 25 to 27,

2. The Crown of Rejoicing (faithfulness in service)

1 Thessalonian 2 vs 19

3.   The Crown of Righteousness (faithfulness in testimony). 11 Timothy 4 v 5 and 8.

4. The Crown of Glory (faithfulness in tending those entrusted to you) 1 Peter 5 vs 2- 4

5. The Crown of Life (faithfulness in temptation and in love). James 1 vs12, Revelation 2 vs 10, 2 Corinthians 5 vs 10

These rewards are worth living for; therefore start TRADING YOUR EARTLY RICHES FOR ETERNAL REWARD.

Appendix

Matthew 10 vs 40 to 42

Matthew 24 vs 31 to 4

FINAL WORD

Thank you for your time.

If the clouds are full of rain, they empty themselves on the earth. The Lord will bless you, bless your bread, bless you farm. In whatever you do, you will prosper. I sense the Lord is bringing you to another realm of prosperity as you get committed to His purpose and emerge a blessing to His kingdom. these are earthly reward and secondly, when we get there, as in when He comes we will receive the eternal reward.

Calm yur heart and receive the word of the Lord: *"behold I am coming quickly and my reward is with me to give to every one according to his work" Revelation 22 vs 12*

Without missing words I believe that you have been changed and prepared to be a blessing to God's Kingdom on earth and to secure eternal reward for yourself. BB.

"I have told you, O man, what is good,
and what the Lord really wants from you…"
Micah 6:8 NET

THE AUTHOR

JOSEPH K. OLUGBOYE is a music educationist turned minister of the Gospel, he is committed to making of disciples through preaching and teaching of God's word with the Lord confirming His word with signs follows.

NATIONALITY: Nigerian

BOOK BY THE SAME AUTHOR: Positioned for Favour

FAMILY LIFE: He is happily married to JOSEH FAITH BIDEMI and the Union is blessed Praise and Emmanuel.

FOR COMMENTS & OBSERVATIONS, PREACHING AND TEACHING ENGAGEMENT OR SPONSORSHIP AND PARTNERSHIP CALL

+234-(0)80-5155-8858

+234-(0)81-3568-5805

E-mail to : pastorojosworld@gmail.com

THE BOOK

HOW MUCH OF EARTHLY RICHES DO YOU HAVE?

Everyone keeps acquiring the earthly riches which the Preacher says "it's vanity upon vanity" and never thinks of securing eternal reward. As good as it sound to be rich here on earth it has no effect on the heavenly home until you deliberately trade it for eternal reward.

Why rich on earth and enter heaven wretched?

Knowing the brevity of man's life, the vanity of the earthly riches and the conviction of eternal home, Joseph Olugboye in his providence writing presents to you how to invest your earthly riches for eternal rewards.

In this book Joseph teaches on the following sub topics among others;-the earthly riches-the incorruptible treasure bank-how to give your earthly riches for eternal reward-Reasons you must invest your earthly riches for eternal rewards.-Earthly and heavenly benefits of trading your earthly riches for eternal reward.

The scriptures says ***"buy the truth and sell it not"*** This book in your hand is the truth you've being waiting for in this side of eternity, I present this book, fully convince that it will help you to invest your earthly riches for eternal reward, make you to enjoy the benefits thereof and prepare you to enter heaven a rich individual.

www.ingramcontent.com/pod-product-compliance
Lightning Source LLC
Chambersburg PA
CBHW021001160726
47994CB00006B/2329